THE UNITED STATES OF WAL-MART

THE UNITED STATES OF

WAL-MART

THE UNITED STATES OF

JOHN DICKER

JEREMY P. TARCHER/PENGUIN

a member of Penguin Group (USA) Inc.

New York

JEREMY P. TARCHER/PENGUIN
Published by the Penguin Group
Penguin Group (USA) Inc., 375 Hudson Street, New York, New York 10014, USA •
Penguin Group (Canada), 10 Alcorn Avenue, Toronto, Ontario M4V 3B2, Canada (a division
of Pearson Penguin Canada Inc.) • Penguin Books Ltd, 80 Strand, London WC2R ORL,
England • Penguin Ireland, 25 St Stephen's Green, Dublin 2, Ireland (a division of Penguin
Books Ltd) • Penguin Group (Australia), 250 Camberwell Road, Camberwell, Victoria 3124,
Australia (a division of Pearson Australia Group Pty Ltd) • Penguin Books India Pvt Ltd,
11 Community Centre, Panchsheel Park, New Delhi–110 017, India • Penguin Group (NZ),
Cnr Airborne and Rosedale Roads, Albany, Auckland 1310, New Zealand (a division of Pearson
New Zealand Ltd) • Penguin Books (South Africa) (Pty) Ltd, 24 Sturdee Avenue,
Rosebank, Johannesburg 2196, South Africa

Penguin Books Ltd, Registered Offices:
80 Strand, London WC2R ORL, England

Most Tarcher/Penguin books are available at special quantity discounts for bulk
purchase for sales promotions, premiums, fund-raising, and educational needs. Special
books or book excerpts also can be created to fit specific needs. For details, write
Penguin Group (USA) Inc. Special Markets, 375 Hudson Street,
New York, NY 10014.

Library of Congress Cataloging-in-Publication Data

Dicker, John, date.
The United States of Wal-Mart / John Dicker.
p.   cm.
Includes bibliographical references and index.
ISBN 1-58542-422-6
1. Wal-Mart (Firm).   2. Discount houses (Retail trade)—United States—
Management.   3. Wages—United States.   4. Employee fringe benefits—
United States.   I. Title.
HF5429.215.U6D53   2005   2005041083
381'.149'0973—dc22

Printed in the United States of America
3   5   7   9   10   8   6   4   2

Book design by Ellen Cipriano
Cover photograph of the author © John Mueller

While the author has made every effort to provide accurate telephone numbers and Internet addresses at
the time of publication, neither the publisher nor the author assumes any responsibility for errors, or for
changes that occur after publication. Further, the publisher does not have any control over and does not
assume responsibility for author or third-party websites or their content.

"Giant Retailer Seeks Hottie with Incentives" was originally published in *Salon*.
Portions of chapter 5 first appeared in a slightly different form in *The Nation*,

CONTENTS

PART TWO:
THE UNITED STATES
OF WAL-MART

GIANT RETAILER SEEKS HOTTIE WITH INCENTIVES

AGE: 42

HOMETOWN: Bentonville, Ark.

OCCUPATION: Behemoth

EDUCATION: $288 billion in annual sales and you care about a degree?

RELIGION: Everyday Low Prices, Cornpone Populism

HEIGHT/WEIGHT: 1.5 million associates in more than 4,906 stores in nine countries on four continents. But I'm not fat, I swear!

HOBBIES: Some days I'm all about squeezing my suppliers; other days all I want to do is cut my payroll. But one thing's for sure: I'm always up for frisbee golf!

TURN-OFFS: Labor unions, zoning laws, and drivers who don't signal.

IN TEN YEARS, I SEE MYSELF . . . Turning $600 billion in annual sales with 20 percent of the domestic retail market, expanding into banking, gas, auto, air travel, healthcare, etc. . . . And hopefully NOT STILL SINGLE!!! LOL

YOU SHOULD GET TO KNOW ME BECAUSE: I will own you.

LAST GREAT BOOK I READ: *Chicken Soup for the Class-Action Defendant's Soul*

CELEBRITY I RESEMBLE MOST: Some say Kmart, others Target. I kinda think Kevin Spacey.

FAVORITE ONSCREEN SEX SCENE: Tie between *Bankrupt Municipalities Gone Wild Vol. 3* and *Porky's* (the shower scene, duh!)

BEST OR WORST LIE I'VE TOLD: "We're not antiunion, we're pro-associate."

IF I COULD BE ANYWHERE AT THE MOMENT I'D BE: Penetrating the fertile markets of India, China, and your heart.

SONG THAT PUTS ME IN THE MOOD: Billboard's Top 20. I know that's vague, but I control 10 percent of domestic music sales.

MOST HUMBLING MOMENT: Kathie Lee Gifford

THE FIVE ITEMS I CAN'T LIVE WITHOUT: My legal team, my political-action committee, politicians acquired through my political-action committee, my satellite-based communications system, and my legal team.

IN MY BEDROOM YOU'LL FIND: Everyday low prices—if you're lucky.

FILL IN THE BLANKS: 1.4 million people screaming your name a letter at a time while wiggling their asses is sexy; Halle Berry doing it at your shareholders' meeting is sexier.

MORE ABOUT ME: Wow, I can't believe I'm actually doing this. All my friends say they don't understand why I'm still single! Anyway, I value honesty, efficiency, and public subsidies. I'm as comfortable running a ballot initiative to circumvent local government authority as I am snuggling up at home with a DVD. I'm fiscally if not socially responsible, hardworking, and I don't sweat the small stuff (provided you've signed an agreement not to sue me).

WHO I'M LOOKING FOR: Call me old-fashioned, but what does a fella have to do to find 20–25 acres on the periphery of a growing exurb? Hello!

While I don't have a type, you have to be near a major regional roadway or interstate or it just won't work out. No head games or mandated economic-impact studies, please.

When responding, please include color photo, all pertinent tax incentives, and signed nondisclosure agreement. Understand that I reserve the right to terminate our relationship at any time based on quarterly same-store sales figures, and that it's totally not personal, OK?

Can't wait to meet you!

THE UNITED STATES OF WAL-MART

THE UNITED STATES
OF WAL-MART

t's hard to say when it became official. Was it was during the 2004 presidential campaign when Dick Cheney sang its praises outside corporate headquarters? Or when Halle Berry showed up in the *New York Times* shaking her groove thang for the company cheer? Perhaps it was after its "plans" for forty new California Supercenters triggered the biggest strike in the state's history, one that resulted in 59,000 grocery workers' swallowing a contract that corrodes their wages, health benefits, and ultimately their unity.

But maybe it was the way its monthly sales figures had become an economic barometer unto themselves. Or perhaps the moment we really knew that things weren't quite right came when we started hearing its propaganda on National Public Radio.

It's hard to know exactly when it happened, just as it's impossible to know when, or if, it will end. But for now it's clear: we're all Wal-Mart's bitches.

If you think this declaration reeks of punk-rock hyperbole, well, maybe you're right; but it's becoming less hyperbolic every thirty-eight hours. That's the rate at which Wal-Mart busts out one of its sprawling Supercenters: a 180,000-to-210,000-square-foot grocery and general merchandise store that does between $100 and $120 million a year in sales. By the end of 2004, there were at least 1,471 of them in the United States alone.[1] Wal-Mart estimates the country can handle another thousand or so before hitting market saturation. Analysts at Merrill Lynch have put the total at more than twice that.[2]

Our ideas of "big corporations" are still rooted in another century, a time when company headquarters were housed in astonishingly tall skyscrapers and where stiff-collared, impeccably dressed white guys made decisions while seated around baronial boardroom tables. These ideas coalesced back when most resources were extracted from the earth, and brawny men with tin lunch pails hammered out products. None of this jibes with the gray box from which you just emerged, with a year's worth of lawn and leaf bags in your shopping cart.

Wal-Mart's statistical pedigrees of retail success are touted so often, and with tones of such envy and awe, that just the numbers alone begin to sound like a mantra of capitalist power prostration. Wal-Mart is . . .

- the largest corporation in the world.
- the largest retailer in the world, hawking more DVDs, magazines, books, CDs, dog food, diapers, bicycles, toys, and toothpaste than any other company.*
- the largest grocer in the world.

*Wal-Mart does not, however, sell the most toilet paper. That distinction goes to its discount competitor Costco.

- owner of the nation's largest private trucking fleet.
- the largest jeweler in the world, with approximately $2.3 billion in sales each year.[3]
- the largest private employer in the United States. And Mexico. And Canada. In fact, more people call it boss than any other private company in the world.
- a country unto itself: if Wal-Mart were an official sovereign nation, its GDP would be larger than that of *80 percent* of the world's countries, including Israel, Ireland, and Sweden.
- the richest company in the world: $288 billion in annual sales. *Billion.* This staggering number marks an increase of $123 billion from only five years earlier, an accomplishment no less incredible since the years were marked by a stock-market collapse, a recession, and topped off by a tepid, jobless recovery.
- by 2007, likely to control 35 percent of all food and drug sales in the United States.[4]
- a corporation that buys more than $1 billion worth of land *each month*.[5]

But no single statistic or analogy sums up Wal-Mart's imperial might. For millions who consider five bucks more than ample lunch money, a number like $288 billion is almost devoid of meaning. It's like staring out the window of an airplane: everything you know as big—eighteen-wheeler trucks, the city skyline, Yao Ming—becomes topographic scribble-scrabble after only a few minutes of steady ascent. Better to focus on the uprightness of your tray table than your own profound smallness.

·   ·   ·

Wal-Mart's CEO, Lee Scott, has often said that none of the company's "world's biggest" distinctions explains why anyone chooses to shop there. He's right. But because Wal-Mart *is* the biggest, it sets the agenda for retailers and a host of dependent industries. Its size and power are the only reasons that hundreds of suppliers have set up offices in or near Wal-Mart's Bentonville, Arkansas, headquarters, making Benton County the otherwise unlikely third-fastest-growing county in the United States. Size and power are what allow Wal-Mart to demand that its suppliers adopt expensive and untested technology that will save Wal-Mart millions from day one but offer no real return on investment for anyone else.

Though it looks like any other "big box" outlet, Wal-Mart has long ceased to be a mere retail chain. It's now as iconic as McDonald's, Coke, and Microsoft. But it isn't just one more arrow in the quiver of big brands. As University of California history professor Nelson Lichtenstein explains, Wal-Mart has become a "template company," an institution whose size and scope sets the tone for the business world at large. In the 1950s, General Motors, then the country's largest corporation, held that distinction. With a gargantuan push from the United Auto Workers, GM established standards for workers' wages, benefits, and the treatment of their unionized employees. These standards were quickly adopted throughout the auto industry, and manufacturing at large, because competitors simply couldn't afford not to follow the template company's lead.

In 1953, the president of GM told the U.S. Congress that "what's good for the United States is good for General Motors, and vice versa." The assertion became famous not just for its moxie, but because it was, arguably, true.[6] If Lee Scott made such a claim today, there'd be the same amount of moxie—maybe more—but it would be maddeningly ironic. General Motors was part of an industry that had never existed before and whose product became part of America's identity, became a metaphor for America itself. More, it created wealth where none existed before. It created high-paying jobs, also known as careers; it abided, for the most part, by the union; it set standards, but it set them high. Its competitors followed GM up; and it didn't force them out of business as much as it demanded better quality from them. GM wasn't a perfect company, nor was it an impeccable social citizen—few corporations truly are. But one could argue that it used its strength and its power for good, not evil.

Wal-Mart's rise has been built on a graveyard of smaller competitors. It has created low-paying jobs. It has not only refused to abide by unions, it hasn't even let them in the door. It has set standards, sure, but it has set them lower, and its competitors have followed Wal-Mart down. Wal-Mart has mastered the art of stocking shelves as cheaply as possible, but with a growing body count and a rap sheet that does not bode well for either American capitalism or America's (and the world's) workers.

And yet we shop there. We shop there a lot. We shop there more than we shop anywhere else. There are reasons for this. Good ones, especially in economically disadvantaged areas where no other retail chains dare to tread, and where the need for cheap, healthy food and staple goods is dire.

But while we may all be Wal-Mart's bitches, we're hardly bending over and barking. For as Wal-Mart grows, so too does the backlash. A fractious lot of workers, property owners, and activists with diverse agendas are holding the company's feet to the fire. But how these anti–Wal-Mart activists can explain to the company's customers—particularly those who, Lee Scott notes, live paycheck to paycheck—why they should pay more at another shop could very well be one of the biggest problems any social movement has ever faced.

. . .

This book is no potboiler, its author popping out of a Dumpster clutching shredded documents that prove the company's nefarious plot to take over the world. And it is certainly no hagiography, a corporate paean of the sort we have started to see more and more of on bookstore shelves. It is, rather, an inquiry into the most powerful company in the country—perhaps in the world—and how its power has changed, and is changing, the way we work, the way we shop, the way we live. It is an examination of how one company has single-handedly altered our expectations of what we deserve as consumers and what we will tolerate as citizens.

Just a hundred years ago, it would have been unthinkable that a retail store could evoke in its customers anything more than a casual sort of loyalty. But there is a war going on. Pitched battles between the forces of economic progress and quality of life, between the preservation of regional identity and national homogeneity, and between the all-important low prices and the dignity of the American worker are beginning to coalesce into an all-out war to define the modern era. And Wal-Mart is winning. It's infiltrated not just the geography of the American landscape, but also the national consciousness. This is an American (and, increasingly, a global) story that has no clear-cut villains or heroes. It's a story that could be the confused, complicated story of America itself.

Welcome to the United States of Wal-Mart.

PART ONE

SIZE
MATTERS

SIZE MATTERS
(NOW MORE THAN EVER)

Unless you've been residing in a national wildlife refuge, you probably hear a lot about Wal-Mart. If you grew up in the company's strongholds—Texas, Florida, Arkansas, Missouri, Oklahoma—you may find it mystifying that an institution that has been around your whole life should suddenly start to trigger so much hysteria. For city dwellers, the mystification occurs in reverse. The city, ahem, is the place where national trends are born, not the sticks. And when these urbanites make their first forays into Wal-Mart, the mystery is no less perplexing. After all, it's just a big, hulking box of concrete masonry unit bricks—cheapest construction material this side of dried dung—structured with steel frames and painted blue and gray with a red racing stripe thrown in for no apparent reason. The cookie-cutter design is square and blunt and ugly enough to make the average inner-city public housing project seem fit for a Vermont ski town.

But beneath the uninspiring exterior is an ecosystem as complex as the Great Barrier Reef. Every second Wal-Mart is open, every transaction is relayed via satellite to the company's very own version of HAL: a 460-terabyte data system housed in its own separate facility two miles from the home office in Bentonville, Arkansas. There, Wal-Mart's data hounds monitor and mine information from its nearly 5,000 locations worldwide. Mastering the sea of information helps it with the little things. (While other retailers merchandise for seasons and holidays, Wal-Mart can adjust its product mix to anticipate oncoming floods and hurricanes.) In a rapidly approaching future, computer chips rigged with tiny radio antennae will allow Wal-Mart to pinpoint the exact location of any product in its global supply chain. When that product reaches the warehouse, the nearest available worker will be informed via PDA as to whether it needs routing for immediate delivery or can go straight to a storage slot.

With or without high tech, Wal-Mart is forever testing and tweaking new ideas. In Dallas, it has crafted a multistory prototype with special escalators rigged to carry shopping carts.* In Lawrence, Kansas, Wal-Mart boasts a "green" store that receives a third of its electrical power from solar panels. It has even spruced up its design to accommodate local tastes: in the resort town of Taos, New Mexico, Wal-Mart has gone adobe; in several Rocky Mountain locales varied rooflines and multicolored masonry brick offer the illusion of big box chalet; and in Fort Worth's Riverside neighborhood it went and added arched windows and a terra-cotta–tiled roof.[1] But the aesthetes at Wal-Mart were not cultivating their creativity organically. The

---

*Wal-Mart can't take credit for this innovation: Target opened a similar store in downtown Minneapolis in October of 2001.

company drew criticism from the communities in which it operated to conform to the local aesthetic. And in some cases it did.

TOYS WERE US

It's like the tired old joke about where at a dinner party an 800-pound gorilla should sit: wherever he wants. With an economy of scale surpassed only by the Almighty, Wal-Mart has King Kong's access to any number of disparate markets. Some of these are less than obvious. For instance, in 2004 it quietly became the nation's leading jeweler.

And now, a moment of silence, please, for Toys "Я" Us. One of the original "category killers," Toys "Я" Us used a discounting strategy of high volume and low prices to gut its competitors, whether humble independents or the toy sections of major department stores. At its height in the mid-nineties, the chain enjoyed 25 percent of the national market. Wal-Mart gobbled that up in less than a decade. With the square footage to devote extra space to seasonal merchandise, and unrivaled purchasing power and distribution capabilities, Wal-Mart became America's number-one toy seller in 1998. In the summer of 2004, Toys "Я" Us formally conceded defeat by announcing it would begin moving away from toys and into its quickly growing Babies "Я" Us division.

The conventional wisdom about competing with Wal-Mart is: don't play their game. Instead, find a behemoth-proof niche. Differentiate or die. And this works for some companies. Porno shops. Um . . . antique stores. Furriers. Gun shops—oh, right, Wal-Mart's rocking that racket, too. So, yeah, Wal-Mart has shown it's eager to identify such nooks and crannies and quickly muscle its way into markets that might, on the face of things, seem unworthy of the effort. With little fanfare, Wal-Mart has entered Internet-oriented businesses like mail-order DVD rentals and pay-to-play music downloads where it undercuts competitor's prices by as much as 10 percent. Wal-Mart also offers check-cashing and money-wiring services at well below the market rate.*

Think Starbucks is bad? In a Plano, Texas, Wal-Mart, "Kicks Coffee" will brew you a latte and hand-deliver it to you in the aisles. Go to Wal-Mart in Birmingham, Alabama, and you can rent a car from Budget. In the Pembroke Pines, Florida, Wal-Mart you can have your towels embroidered at "Hometown Threads."

Its expansive parking lots are host to hundreds of gas stations: some of them Wal-Mart owns; but most are contracted out to third-party operators. Instead of profiting on the gas, Wal-Mart collects rent and banks on the increased customer traffic the stations generate. Only when you're a true colossus can petroleum serve as your dancing monkey.

Experimentation is ingrained in Wal-Mart's DNA; as Sam Walton was known to quip, "Try it, do it, improve it." But for every Supercenter model there's more than a few forgotten flops. Helen's Arts and Crafts stores, named after Walton's wife, were abandoned in the late eighties. In the early nineties Wal-Mart dabbled in a farm supply store as well as a hybrid discount operation called "Bud's Warehouse Outlets." These peddled damaged goods and product overruns at major discounts in locations where abandoned Wal-Marts couldn't wriggle out of their leases.

The truth is that nobody outside Bentonville knows exactly what

---

*It's tough to feel sympathy for the "little guy" in this case, as the check-cashing industry profits almost exclusively from those too poor to open a checking account. By undercutting the competition, Wal-Mart is certainly acting in its own self-interest (where else but inside one of its stores would Wal-Mart want to unleash freshly paid poor people?), but it is undoubtedly saving poor people money.

Wal-Mart will do next; but since the 1980s each decade has seen it deploy at least one new prototype that has helped it enter or solidify a new market segment. In 1983 it launched its first Sam's Club wholesale discount store. Five years later it entered the grocery game with its first Supercenter. And in 1998 it launched Neighborhood Market. At a mere 40,000 square feet, these food-mostly stores were hyped by industry observers as Wal-Mart's golden chariot into urban markets. So far, however, the deployment has been modest, or at least modest by Wal-Mart standards, with ten to fifteen new stores per year.*

Despite being a power in the United Kingdom and a presence in Germany, Wal-Mart plays international second fiddle to the French-owned Carrefour chain, which operates in twenty-nine European and Asian countries. Many of these are markets in which Wal-Mart has yet to establish a beachhead. Wal-Mart is also taking its sweet time in the highly saturated retail markets of Japan and South Korea. When the world is your target market, there's plenty of room for growth. As Lee Scott has said, "All we want to do is grow."[2]

Wal-Mart remains the largest private employer in the United States, its largest retailer, its largest grocery store—and the largest corporation in the world. From Sega Genesis to Huggies, from DVDs to a Happy Meal and an oil change, all this can be yours with a single visit to a Wal-Mart Supercenter. In a county of zealous "stuff-lovers," no one distributes as much of it as the Arkansas-based retail empire does.

As Wal-Mart has grown, leaving its rival Kmart in a blue light

---

*Small or Supercenter-sized, Wal-Mart takes its time with new models. While the first Supercenter opened in 1988, after five years it only had a total of thirty. By 1997, however, it was up to 344. Whether Neighborhood Market is set to blow up on a similar scale remains to be seen; but its slow-but-steady growth through its first five years is eerily similar to that of the Supercenter.

of bankruptcy, this imperial corporation has earned the enmity of thousands of Americans and has become, rightly or not, the apotheosis of a laundry list of social ills: suburban sprawl, the decline of the distinct downtown commercial center, the increased dependence on overseas sweatshops, poverty wages, keeping people in the no-man's-land of making too much money to qualify for assistance but too little to afford private health insurance. Yet, despite a series of public humiliations, well-covered by the media—including its phony "Buy America" campaign and the Kathie Lee Gifford sweatshop scandal—Wal-Mart has not only persevered, it has grown stronger. It continues to grow by 275 Supercenters per year, not to mention those gross revenues of roughly $288 billion a year.

What will be left in the wake of Wal-Mart's continued domination? What does this domination mean for small businesses, citizens and workers? At what point will Wal-Mart become a monopoly—or has it already become a monopoly? Is Wal-Mart killing us softly with our own song? And if so, can we do anything about it?

"RAY, KMART SUCKS!"

There was no eyewitness, no smoking gun or stained dress, so let's just say it all began, or ended, at the movies. The year was 1988, and Tom Cruise and Dustin Hoffman were together on screen for the first time, an event that, at the time, was nearly as exciting as a Michael Dukakis photo op. It was not your typical midlife-crisis movie, but it was close enough: cocky Los Angeles car salesman learns to love again through enforced proximity to an idiot savant who just so happens to be the brother he never knew he had. On a cross-country road trip, nascent bonding is thrown for a loop when Cruise can't quite deal with his brother's fervent literalisms and religiosity toward routine: *The People's Court* at 4:30; eight (not four) fish sticks for dinner; no airplanes; and no driving in the rain. But what forces Cruise to pull off the road and desecrate the open prairie with a torrent of obscenities is his brother's insistence that his dwindling supply of underwear can only be replenished from one place. In a hopeless quest to impart a modicum of sartorial discernment, Cruise yells: "Ray, Kmart sucks!"

And that was it: the last great hurrah of unabashed discount-store snobbery. Even if today's 'tween-age girls still suffer the occasional slander about their wardrobe being derived from a "mart," the shame in discount shopping is becoming more archaic every second.

Whether it's Target's carefully honed aura of discount chic, Costco's grab bag of who-knows-what, or Wal-Mart itself, Americans have become inordinately proud of getting a bargain. Everyone and their mother—*especially* their mother—claims the mantle of "Wal-Mart Queen" or "Costco King." The intense satisfaction in relaying blow-by-blow accounts of saving three dollars on a salmon fillet has become like a junkie's fix. One wonders at what point it will become perfectly normal to hang a framed receipt next to daguerreotypes of the family patriarchs. The duration and detail of such narratives are enough to make one question whether they're really about a simple purchase. It's as if a moral victory has been won when you get a deal, as if a battle has been fought and you have vanquished the retail demon by getting a few cents off your Maxwell House. The Wal-Mart ethos has slowly been penetrating our consumer consciousness, cooing into the shopper's ear that discounting is actually a system of near-religious morality: Yes, you totally deserve the lowest prices, even if employees get screwed on wages and suppliers have to outsource in order to get you those prices. Relax, you deserve it.

EGO-INTENSIVE BARRIERS

It's hard to imagine "Kmart sucks" flying in the age of "Wal-Mart Republicans." Never mind that the store once mighty and strong has now merged with fellow convalescing giant Sears in hopes of surviving Wal-Mart. The way Americans shop has undergone a seismic shift.

"The ego-intensive barriers are no longer there anymore to prevent people from surfing other areas," explains *Retail Forward*'s apparel analyst Lois Huff. And with the stigma scrubbed off the cultural permission slips to shop, new images of how the other half lives arrive at a steady clip. Ivana Trump tells the *New York Times Magazine* she's cuckoo for Costco, even if she doesn't exactly know what kind of deal she (and her chef) are actually getting; Sarah Jessica Parker, whose *Sex and the City* character wouldn't be caught dead in anything less than Blahniks, is only too happy to tell Conan about her $12.99 Target pajamas. And a *New York Times* fashion writer fesses up that she shops Wal-Mart for the prices *and* the styles.

So what exactly drove down the "ego-intensive barriers"? Certainly not a Tom Cruise backlash, as welcome as that might be. It's hard to pinpoint any one event or trend; rather, it was a confluence of economic declines and advancements in technology that helped change how and where we shop. For starters, the economic recession of the early 1990s was one of the first to feature large numbers of white-collar workers losing their jobs as corporations underwent major restructuring to stay competitive with Japan. But as things were getting uglier on the outside, inside the stores the outlook was far sunnier. The products once widely written off as garbage were becoming a lot less sucky.

In the mid-eighties Kmart followed Sears' lead by crafting an in-house clothing line endorsed by former Charlie's Angel Jaclyn Smith. A bit of attention to aesthetics and a widening in sizes for the ballooning American waistline and Kmart had a runaway hit, one Wal-Mart quickly copied with an even less threatening celeb named Kathie Lee Gifford.

It wasn't just clothing that was getting better, but higher-end merchandise as well. Boom boxes and VCRs, clock radios and kitchen appliances were all showing up on the shelves with name brands and low prices. Veteran retail consultant Ira Kalish, now with the investment firm Deloitte & Touche, argues that quality improvements have eroded much of the former reverence for the high-end chains and brands.

"The majority of consumers believe that apparel is as good at discounters as it is at department stores." And with electronics, any number of brands provide good quality. "It used to be that if you wanted a good TV you had to get a Sony; that's no longer true."[3]

And the stores continued to multiply as every product category gave birth to twins, if not triplets. In athletic gear there were Sports Authority, Galyans, and Gart; for electronics Best Buy and Circuit City; homebodies enjoyed Bed, Bath & Beyond and the odiously named Linens N' Things. Books went to Borders and to Barnes & Noble; home improvement to Home Depot; pet supplies found homes at Petsmart and Petco; and on and on and on.

Most of these stores adhered to similar discounting formulas of high volume and low prices, though with an emphasis on selection, the cost pressure was less intense than it was on the general merchandiser. Though not quite Supercenter size, these big boxes set up in the same parking-rich environments on the suburban fringe. While the category killers and the discount generalists flourished, the middle began to contract. Small businesses in these categories were forced to radically differentiate themselves or perish. Finding themselves hosed on price and merchandising, middlebrow department stores like JC Penney and Sears were also forced to rethink their game. Indicative of how severely they were being pinched, in the nineties, both chains threw in the towel on cosmetics, a department-store staple.

As category killers sucked the wind out of retail categories like books, pet supplies, and sporting goods, markets comprised largely of middle-ground goods started claiming the higher end of the spectrum. With track lighting, hardwood floors, and well-groomed staff, J. Crew, Abercrombie & Fitch, Urban Outfitters, Anthropologie, Off Fifth, and others found niches of those willing to pay more for something between style and status. The grocery game witnessed its own frou-frouing as chains like Whole Foods, Wild Oats, and Bread & Circus brought hippie health-food-store products to a larger format with an emphasis on customer service and presentation.

With a shop for every possible demographic and product category, the sheer volume of chains has made it increasingly difficult to shop anywhere else. At the same time, the emergence of online retailers offered another set of price pressures. Sites like Amazon, Overstock, drugstore.com, and eBay are not only competition for retailers, they also provide consumers with quick educations. Gone are the days when buying a new TV meant traipsing to the library for the relevant issue of *Consumer Reports*. Now sites like Amazon feature dozens of reviews on every imaginable product, written, at least in theory, by those who've taken the purchase plunge. Armed with Internet ammo, there's hardly anything the consumer can't demand anymore.

ALL THINGS TO ALL PEOPLE, ALL THE TIME

The growth in retail space in America has outpaced that of population. In 1986, 28,496 shopping centers combined for 3.5 billion square feet of U.S. retail space. In 2003, the totals grew to 46,438 malls and 5.8 billion square feet. According to the National Research Bureau's shopping-center census, retail square footage per American has increased by 37 percent since 1987.[4]

As stores grow more ubiquitous they've made a bid to become all things to all people. This has nothing to do with magnanimity but rather involves keeping bodies in the building, as studies show the longer customers stay, the more they spend (the same logic that keeps clocks off walls in bars and casinos). Most Wal-Mart Supercenters are human service stations unto themselves, like a Middle Eastern market, but without that pesky human interaction.

Under one roof a customer can buy groceries and goods, process film, receive an oil change or even rent a car, get a haircut, an eye exam, passport photos, cash their paycheck, and choose from fine dining options like McDonald's, Krispy Kreme, and Wal-Mart's very own Radio Grill snack bar. Walk into a Target Supercenter and stare across the great American palate divide with Starbucks and sushi on one side of the sliding doors and Taco Bell and Pizza Hut on the other. Many Walgreens pharmacies now stock food, including produce. And nearly all discount retailers and chain groceries have their own pharmacy. With so many choices at our disposal, general retailers can't afford to lose out on anything.

NO LOGO? NO PROBLEM!

We've all seen them. In between paychecks, we've all shamefacedly dragged the "cheapo" private-label soda or detergent or cornflakes up to the counter. Well, be shamefaced no more. Private-label merchandise is the new black.

Less visible than the circus tent of in-store food and services, but far more indicative of why Kmart sucketh less, is the explosion in private-label merchandise. Also known as "generics" or "economy," their lifeless packaging gave the impression of having been remaindered from an Eastern bloc commissary. Years ago only the basic staples, what some retail wonks refer to as "low-emotional involvement goods,"[5] such as flour, sugar, and butter, would be packaged under private labels.

After a slow and painful discovery that consumers weren't willing to trade quality for price, manufacturers began improving to the point where, in many cases, the only thing separating private labels from the glossy brands is a marketing budget. And that's the golden ticket: by doffing promotions and advertising, private labels (PLs) let retailers cut prices 25 percent below competition with as much as a 10 percent improvement in profit margins. Pricing, improved quality, and packaging that no longer carries a stigma have all made PLs more prolific. Between 1998 and 2004, PLs grew at more than double the rate of branded goods.[6] One of the most successful lines is Costco's Kirkland signature, which appears on everything from patio heaters to olive oil. In a quick five-year period ending in 2003, the discount chain added 400 different items to the line. The brand now comprises 12 percent of Costco's total sales.[7]

Lest one conclude that PLs are only carving a fruitful niche in the "it'll do" genre, dig this: between 1997 and 2003, the number of product categories in which PLs were the number-one seller across the board shot up by 55 percent. In the case of Costco, its Kirkland cranberry juice and lawn and leaf bags outsold the national brands in its own stores to the point where the company decided it wasn't worth stocking their brand-name competitors at all.[8]

As often as they're lumped together, likening Wal-Mart to Costco is like confusing polar bears with applesauce. Well, maybe they have more in common than that, but not as much as one might think. Costco can boot a few brands because it has carefully positioned itself to its customers as a shopping treasure hunt: what's there today might not be tomorrow. In this context, impulse buys masquerade as common sense.

But the real kicker is that despite its size, Costco has a lot less "stuff." Its total arsenal of products, or stock keeping units (SKUs) as they're known, is approximately 4,000. Wal-Mart's typically exceeds 100,000.[9] But because it has the floor space and a broader customer base, Wal-Mart is in a unique position when it comes to brands. Some of its in-house lines have grown so popular that their status on the shelves has become a question of marketing ontology: are they private labels or actual brand-name goods? Certainly Wal-Mart's Faded Glory apparel, Mary Kate and Ashley 'tween wear, and Sam's Choice beverages can now be considered brands. But no private label has succeeded more epically than Ol' Roy dog food. Named after one of Walton's hunting dogs (one that couldn't hunt, as it turned out) Ol' Roy has become the nation's best-selling dog food, outpacing Pedigree and Purina by an annual margin of more than 20 percent,[10] a remarkable feat considering the brand is only available at Wal-Mart.

In other areas, Wal-Mart is able to use its private-label prowess to outmuscle national brands yet still keep them begging the company to be stocked. Such was the case with Ocean Spray. Establishing a Bentonville office enabled the company to get the advance skinny on Wal-Mart's merchandising plans and then quickly step in to fill the need. As a result, its sales at the retailer shot up by 11 percent. But what Wal-Mart giveth, it's only too happy to taketh away. Just a year after Ocean Spray debuted a sixty-four-ounce jug of white cranberry juice to be sold at Wal-Mart for $2.50, out came an identical version from the Sam's Choice line for only $1.98.[11] Here's where suppliers eat an insult-and-injury value meal—bringing their price down to the level Wal-Mart demands, only to get burned later.

The PL push is not just limited to juice and dog chow. At Wal-Mart, a forty-two-inch plasma television sells below $2,000, a recordable DVD player for less than $150, and an LCD monitor for $278. All private label, all at a fraction of the brand-name price.[12]

Because of its enormity Wal-Mart comfortably absorbs both private labels and brands. It's not a happy fit for everyone, but until customers decide to dispense with brands altogether, there's still a market to be served. But that market is shrinking, and in that respect, things look good for Wal-Mart. *Private Label* magazine estimates that store brands made up 40 percent of Wal-Mart's sales in 2003. Other estimates put the number at half as much.

In 1964, long before Sam's Choice sodas and Ol' Roy dog chow were even a glimmer in daddy's eye, Sam Walton conducted a test. He had just opened his second Wal-Mart in Harrison, Arkansas, and it was an ugly one: it was cramped with eight-foot ceilings and rickety with wooden plank fixtures.

"It was just barely put together," Walton wrote of it later. The store looked particularly run-down compared to its competitor in town—a store with nice lighting, sturdy, clean floors, and the rest of the trimmings of a well-appointed retail space. But the in-town store's prices were 20 percent higher. The test was, as Walton explained, to discover "if customers in a town of 6,000 people would come to our kind of barn and buy the same merchandise strictly because of price. The answer was yes."[13]

THE STORY THAT WON'T DIE

In an age of global terrorism and preemptive war it may seem strange that a chain of discount stores should keep finding its way into the news. In 2003 the *Los Angeles Times* bagged a Pulitzer Prize for a three-part series on the chain's global influence. The *New York Times* has told of workers being locked inside stores overnight, of its use of illegal immigrants, and its effects on book and magazine publishing. The *Wall Street Journal* has provided some of the most rigorous Wal-Mart coverage, on everything from the company's health-care plan to the growing power of its Washington lobby. And state and regional papers have all chimed in with their own versions of "Dude, where's my neighborhood grocer?"

BusinessWeek wonders, "Is Wal-Mart Too Powerful?" *Fortune* asks, "Should We Admire Wal-Mart?" *The Economist* claims that it's "Learning to Love Wal-Mart"; *Fast Company* tells us about "The Wal-Mart You Don't Know." According to *Forbes,* "Sam Walton Made Us a Promise." And outlets far too numerous to name have been unable to resist some version of "Up Against the Wal."

Each week brings fresh outrages. In the month of September 2004, Wal-Mart opened a store on the site of an ancient tribal burial ground on the Hawaiian island of Maui. The same year, Wal-Mart announced plans to plop a Supercenter at San Juan Teotihuacán, northeast of Mexico City—a Supercenter that would be visible from the top of nearby ancient pyramids. (The announcement triggered multiple hunger strikes.)

Given all this coverage, it's easy to forget that to most people, Wal-Mart is *just* a store. A place to buy batteries, dog food, and paper towels to a soundtrack of barcode blips and infant apoplexy. As former *Atlantic Monthly* columnist and author Thomas Hine notes, "Never before has so much been available to so many. And never before has it seemed so dull."[14]

Harp too long on Wal-Mart and people may want to know if it's really that bad. What about all the Targets, Kohl's, Home Depots, Costcos, Kmarts, Petsmarts, Office Maxes, Whole Foods, Best Buys, Circuit Citys, and BJ's Wholesale Clubs? Why isn't anyone talking about them? They have to be doing something wrong, right? That so many news outlets should be so consumed with one company's doings suggests either an outbreak of monomania or, as some have claimed, a political agenda.

One reason Wal-Mart is a story as fixed in the news cycle as the war on terrorism is apparent in the second paragraph of every article written about it: Wal-Mart is big. It's so big it takes several paragraphs just to catalogue its bigness. As predictable as these second paragraphs have become, it is difficult to understate the company's scope. Consider:

- Wal-Mart alone represents a staggering 2 percent of the GDP of the United States of America.
- Wal-Mart employs one out of every 115 American workers.
- Wal-Mart is more than four times the size of its largest retail rival, Home Depot.

Other stores may look and feel and behave in similar ways, but comparing why they're treated differently in the media is like asking why Britney is always in *Us Weekly* instead of the third runner-up on *American Idol*. As much as Wal-Mart might smell like the media's flavor of the month, the avalanche of stories does not reflect an ephemeral interest.

But what gives the Wal-Mart story legs is more than impressive statistics. As *The New Yorker*'s Ken Auletta writes, the mainstream media are not so much biased toward a political camp as they are toward conflict itself. And Wal-Mart has provided enough scandals, lawsuits, and irresistible storylines to keep journalists busy for years beyond the rapture.

When Wal-Mart first blipped on the public's radar, the narrative, however nascent, was framed as a feel-good story, in which the main character was a good ol' boy from Arkansas, the quixotic figure of Sam Walton. Despite being the country's richest man, he drove a beater pickup, flew coach class, and got five-dollar haircuts. The concept of the "backwoods billionaire" was new, intriguing, and, perhaps most important, it appealed to a nation that, although growing increasingly cynical, still celebrated the self-made man.

As Walton's company became a national powerhouse, spreading beyond the Ozarks and the Sunbelt, skirmishes erupted between the company and the communities it served, between the company and the states in which it operated, between the company and a vociferous and growing antiglobalization movement, and even between the company and its employees. All of this attracted media attention, and the story was too good to drop. The more the media investigated, the more conflict it uncovered. It's nearly impossible to cite all the ongoing battles in this escalating war between Wal-Mart and the media. A few of the most notorious:

- the "mom-and-pop" shops versus the corporate behemoth that puts them out of business
- the popularity of low prices versus the unpopularity of their social costs
- First World consumers versus Third World producers
- union solidarity versus the "the Wal-Mart family"
- blue-state quaint versus red-state pragmatic
- retail spaces that are big, cheap, and no-frills versus those that are small, distinct, and where, at least in theory, everybody *could* know your name

Not all of these oppositions are as binary as presented, but they offer convenient frameworks on which stories can be built and then published—again and again and again. But is this bad? Is it antibusiness to ask questions about a company's business practices? And if it's not, then what, exactly, is the point to these stories? To change policy? To change consumers' minds? Maybe Wal-Mart is just a convenient target, a very visible corporate villain whose success is the very thing that people hate about it. Or maybe the company represents an unstoppable force in American capitalism, one that is destined to erase regional identity by giving every state in the union the Wal-Mart Makeover.

It's hard to know what the real story is, because the real story is complicated.

A MACRO-SIZED MICROCOSM

Wal-Mart serves as a macro-sized microcosm of many of America's biggest socioeconomic clusterfucks. Take the ongoing loss of American manufacturing jobs to China, Bangladesh, India, and beyond. A result of new technology and the global marketplace, and spurred by that "retro" conflict between labor and capital, outsourcing has decimated the U.S. manufacturing base, which has been hemorrhaging jobs for seven straight years. Wal-Mart didn't start this trend; and because it relies mostly on suppliers and subcontractors rather than foreign firms directly, the company's hands usually stay clean. As Lee Scott told the *Wall Street Journal* in 2004, "I am not familiar with the idea that Wal-Mart brings anyone in and says you need to take this item offshore. I can't say it never happened, but I can say that is not our policy."[15]

As the CEO suggests, no Bentonville buyer is ever going to whisper the equivalent to "Michigan bad, Guangdong Province good!" in a supplier's ear. That's because they don't have to. It's no secret the company plays hardball with its suppliers (from whom

Bentonville's buyers are forbidden from accepting so much
drink). Not only do the buyers demand the lowest price, as any business would, they also require seven to eight "points of improvement"
a year. These can range from adding cost efficiencies to their supply
line to more consistent sizing on garments. They're burdensome, and
sometimes next to impossible to achieve: Wal-Mart's demands make
it difficult for its suppliers to offer their employees livable wages and
good working conditions—not when you've got the world's largest
retailer holding your leash.

Wal-Mart is the pimp who owns all the strolls: if you don't play
the game, you might as well go back home to Wichita. No official
"policy" is necessary when the writing is already on the wall.

Then there's the ubiquity of Wal-Mart itself, the way it is altering the American landscape. Conservatives have argued that the
building of Wal-Marts and Supercenters in economically depressed
areas is *the solution* for urban blight. In a column on the alternative
news website "The Raw Story," columnist Brian Holley wonders if
the Wal-Marts that are popping up in urban areas, where lower-
income families seek out low-price goods, are like the pox-infested
blankets freshly landed Europeans gave to Native Americans. Great
in the short term; devastating over time. The very concept of "sprawl"
evokes visions of Wal-Mart, as the typical Supercenter requires a
twenty-plus-acre lot—space for a thousand parking spots—and generates an estimated 7,000 to 10,000 car trips per day.

And a widely publicized report from Good Jobs First, a nonprofit think tank, revealed that the federal and state governments
have subsidized Wal-Mart to the tune of nearly $4 billion. These
subsidies come in a rainbow of colors: free or reduced-price land, tax
breaks, sales tax rebates, state corporate income tax credits, and so
on. The other subsidy that Wal-Mart receives from the government
is endorsement for its near-poverty wages: the amount of money

Wal-Mart employees and their dependents cost the states in which they operate in welfare benefits, which many workers rely on to make ends meet, numbers in the hundreds of millions of dollars—per year. The Good Jobs First report estimated that a full 90 percent of all Wal-Marts and Supercenters built on U.S. soil receive some kind of government subsidy.

But while it seems Wal-Mart has become a public-subsidy crack whore, have Americans become crack whores for Wal-Mart?

WE PROVIDE JOBS!

For the depressed communities that Wal-Mart approaches, invariably the carrot is the promise of jobs and more jobs. And yet one of the most widely and publicly leveled charges against Wal-Mart is that, better adjectives notwithstanding, its jobs suck. In 2004 the company claimed that a full-time worker averaged $9.64 per hour, up from only $8.27 two years earlier. Since full time is thirty-two hours a week, the average annual take-home pay totals around $18,000 a year (assuming hours aren't cut, as they often are). For a family of four, the figure is nearly a thousand dollars *below* the poverty line.[16] Add to this that Wal-Mart's health insurance is priced so far beyond the reach of most of its associates that states from Washington to Georgia have found the company's workers to be among the largest groups seeking public assistance, and Wal-Mart's carrot begins to look like a very meager meal.

Hardly a season goes by without a new Wal-Mart scandal: 2,000 illegal immigrants working for subminimum wages as janitors; workers on overnight shifts are locked inside stores; lawsuits in twenty-eight states alleging unpaid overtime on behalf of thousands of current and former workers. And the real doozy: a class-action lawsuit alleging systematic gender discrimination against 1.6 million female workers. When certified in the spring of 2004 it became the largest civil rights lawsuit in American history. In fact, it is estimated that Wal-Mart faces roughly 5,000 lawsuits each year,[17] an average of about thirteen new suits *each day*.

Workers who so much as dabble in union organizing are subjected to surveillance by management and onslaughts of antiunion meetings, videos, and reprisals. When workers have managed to persevere and elect union representation, Wal-Mart has responded by eliminating entire job classifications, and threatening to close stores.[18]

When confronted with this information, the company response is: "Wal-Mart provides good jobs." It's like some sort of corporate mantra designed to soothe troubled souls and put worried minds at ease. Wait: I can't make ends meet on this wage. *Wal-Mart provides good jobs.* But the deductible is 42 percent of my yearly salary; I can't afford that. *Wal-Mart provides good jobs.*

The hypnotist act works well on desperate communities with high unemployment numbers. They don't need too much convincing. The message is clear: You need us more than we need you.

"We opened a store last year in Valley Stream [a Long Island suburb just across the border from New York City] where we had over 15,000 applicants for 300 jobs," Michael Duke, CEO of the Wal-Mart Stores division said in spring of 2004. "They all wanted to wear that Wal-Mart badge. When I visit with our associates, I can see their pride. They know they were the very best from more than 15,000 applicants. They feel like the chosen ones."[19]

The hordes of applicants don't merely want a job; they want a Wal-Mart job. As a pleased-as-pork Lee Scott told an industry panel about a store opening in Phoenix, "We had 500 job openings, we had

5,000 applications. Maybe it is different where you live, but where we live, people don't line up to get a new job that pays less and has less benefits. The world does not work that way."

Except when it does. Wal-Mart's moral calculus is a strange hybrid of know-nothing and spin: the stock market fallout of 2000, the slow recession that veered dangerously close to a minor depression after September 11, and a recovery unprecedented in the amount of jobs it *didn't* create played no role in the formation of Wal-Mart's rationale for continuing business as usual despite the bad press. And though few call the company out on such twisted logic, Wal-Mart's claim that the number of applicants for its jobs reflects the quality of its jobs is like saying soup-kitchen lines are a referendum on soup.

From executives like Duke and Scott, the overriding message is: Trust us. Even if our associates make a fraction of our annual bonuses, hey, we *know* them and they *love* it.

"People who write about the quality of jobs at Wal-Mart don't understand or know anything about our associates," Duke explains. "When you get to know our people, their dedication and loyalty, and you see firsthand their level of commitment, you realize these are quality jobs."[20]

But don't take it from Duke. Lee Scott, whose 2003 salary and bonus (including stock grants of $17.4 million) was 966 times the salary of a full-time associate explains it this way: "It is not forced labor. The truth is, I go to the stores and shake hands with the associates, and they like working at Wal-Mart."[21]

More than 500,000 associates leave Wal-Mart each year. In fact, the company's 2003 turnover rate of 44 percent was actually the *lowest* it had seen in recent years. Just two years earlier, it was churning through over 56 percent of its employees annually. Within the first ninety days of employment, when the majority of turnover occurs, the figure was a staggering 70 percent. Even at its current "low" of 44 percent, with a roster of 1.2 million associates, Wal-Mart must hire 660,000 fresh bodies a year just to maintain homeostasis.

STORYTELLING

The consensus in Bentonville is that times have changed. Wal-Mart, they say, *must* do a better job of using the media to tell its story. However, for much of its history, Wal-Mart didn't need the media. Unlike an Internet start-up (remember those?) or a Tina Brown publication (remember that?), no "buzz" is required to get people into its stores. While it'll often christen a new store with a pep rally, complete with marching bands, cheerleaders, and other wholesome incarnations of American rah rah rah, these fêtes are not intended to draw media attention or trigger sales. With the exception of certain hotel heiresses, everybody has heard of Wal-Mart.

But times have changed for Wal-Mart. Its anonymity is gone, as is its underdog status. Unflattering and unfortunate episodes that might have fallen by the wayside in Sam Walton's day will now make fast headlines. But implicit in the oft-stated presumption that effective storytelling is all that's required is the idea that if more people could just understand *the real Wal-Mart,* and not the one portrayed in the newspapers and TV, perhaps have a Massengill moment with a smiling associate or two, then its unaffordable health insurance, low wages, and cutthroat business practices would dissolve into the ether.

In January of 2005, Lee Scott went on the offensive against the company's critics. Taking out more than one hundred full-page newspaper ads trumpeting the company's wages and benefits, Scott told the Associated Press that he felt Wal-Mart was being "nibbled to death by guppies."

"We're taking this time to say, 'Hold on a minute, we have good jobs,'" he said.[22] Scott intended to spread this good news through a series of planned meetings with various organizations in which he vowed to explain Wal-Mart's labor practices, its environmental policies, and the way it conducts business with its suppliers. He refused to name the organizations.

"If you're a company with a budget the size of Wal-Mart and you're claiming to be misunderstood, it's pretty pathetic frankly," says PR consultant and industry analyst Paul Holmes, who sees Wal-Mart's PR efforts as being quick and cosmetic in nature. "It's a lot easier to get a face-lift than to change your whole personality, or change your character."

It might be hard to believe, but critical press is not always the result of bad or inadequate PR, or an ideological agenda. Sometimes unflattering stories can actually come from unflattering facts. As a *New York Times* editorial put it, "If Wal-Mart wants to do a better job in telling its story, it needs to work on having a better story to tell."[23]

But for now, at least, the story isn't pretty.

TWO

"MOST VERSATILE BOY": HOW SAM WALTON BECAME AN ETHOS

I believe our way of looking at things is going to
come into its own in this decade and the next century.
The way business is conducted worldwide is going to be
different, and a lot of that difference is going to reflect
what we egotistically think of as the Wal-Mart way.

—SAM WALTON, *MADE IN AMERICA*

I n the fall of 1945, as most of America waxed orgasmic over
Hirohito's surrender and the end of World War II, a young shop-
keeper in a small Arkansas town had other, more pressing matters
on his mind: panties.

With $20,000 borrowed from his father-in-law and another
$5,000 from his wife, Sam Walton was the proud proprietor of a Ben
Franklin five-and-dime in the town of Newport. A rapidly growing
franchise chain in the postwar era, Ben Franklins were a staple of
southern and midwestern towns too small to merit a Woolworth's. In
much the same way a Tastee-Freeze (and not a Dairy Queen) confirms
a town's Podunk bona fides, a Ben Franklin was an indispensable detail
in the portrait of small-town life that Americans held so dear. The

stores carried a host of low-ticket items ranging from games and toys to health and beauty items to seasonal mishmash.

Butler Brothers, the Chicago-based corporation that owned Ben Franklin, allowed anyone entry into the merchant game, assuming some start-up capital. It even provided merchant newbies a primer covering everything from pricing to payroll. This not only helped to acclimate the newbies, it also ensured a uniformity of products, procedures, and profits.[1] To Walton, however, the Butler Brothers manual was only a springboard, not a bible. He had other plans.

Butler Brothers required Walton, as it required all Ben Franklin operators, to purchase 80 percent of his stock from the company's warehouses. Walton chafed at this. He started sniffing out other arrangements. Most wholesalers Walton approached were skittish about selling directly to him, fearful of the repercussions from cutting Butler Brothers out of the picture. However, he did persuade an unfortunately named New Yorker, one Harry Weiner, to supply him with satin, elastic-waist panties for two bucks a dozen: 25 percent less than he was paying Butler Brothers. As Walton would later note in his autobiography: "If you're interested in, 'How Wal-Mart did it,' this is one story you've got to sit up and pay close attention to."[2]

With Weiner's cheap panties, Walton could mark down from his Butler Brothers price of three for a dollar to a pack of four for the same price. As the panties flew out the door, volume begat profits that wouldn't have existed without the low price. Panty-ology was only the first success in a strategy Walton would later dub EDLP (Everyday Low Prices). Buy low, sell low, and as a result sell more. As another famous Arkansan might have put it, "It's the volume, stupid." In the 1940s, Walton had no idea just how powerful this concept could be, but the seed had been planted.

Far more pressing for Walton at the time were the daily details of storekeeping. He innovated: setting a popcorn machine outside and hoping its aroma would draw passersby into the store. When that proved successful, Walton took out an $1,800 loan for a soft-serve ice cream machine. Seems like kid stuff; but in 1940s Arkansas, such ploys bordered on the transgressive.

According to Walton's brother Bud, retailing in the Sun Belt was then comprised of state-based fiefdoms. Ben Franklins were the bottom-feeders, filling in the spaces left between larger stores.

"Oklahoma was TG&Y," Bud said in *Made in America,* "Kansas was Alco, Texas was Motts, Missouri was Mattingly. Nebraska was Hested's. Indiana was Danners. They were locally based and developed and they'd say, 'Well, you don't cross my border and I won't cross your border.' . . . Borders didn't mean much to my brother."[3] Every bit as much as his work ethic, this sort of border-crossing—whether it be crossing state lines to get better deals on cheap merchandise or trampling over long-established business practices—is what made Walton a visionary.

"In many of my core values—things like church and family and civic leadership and even politics—I'm a pretty conservative guy," Walton wrote, "but for some reason, in business, I have always been driven to buck the system. . . ."[4]

As a Ben Franklin franchisee in the postwar era, "bucking the system" meant cutting deals with small wholesalers, often driving long hours to Tennessee warehouses. There he'd stuff his hitched "Jon boat" trailer full of whatever was cheap and had a chance of selling. Walton also made a point of keeping competition in check even when it was more trouble than it was worth. For instance, as Walton's Newport store became more and more successful word got out that his competitor John Dunham wanted to expand into a building that had just been vacated by a Kroger grocery store. The same day Walton heard the news, he scooped it out from under Dunham. (Walton wanted the space for a small "department" store, which he admitted functioned mainly in keeping his competition at bay.)

Only five years after opening his first five-and-dime, Walton had turned his Ben Franklin into the largest variety store in Arkansas. With $250,000 in annual sales, it was the most profitable Ben Franklin in the six-state region.

There may have been something addictive, as well as instructive, in this experience. The innovations had worked. The shrewdness had paid off. And there was an entire country full of Ben Franklins that could use Walton's expert hand. Hoarding was something that Walton, Dust Bowl baby that he was, might have considered a survival strategy. As anyone with a grandparent who lived through the Depression knows, it's hard for someone who has known want to know when it is safe to stop hoarding. Walton, it seems, was never quite certain he would never "go hungry" again.

LET US NOW FORECLOSE
ON FAMOUS MEN

However much damage identity politics and multiculturalism have inflicted on the "Great White Male" school of American history, it hasn't touched the myth of Sam Walton. And it is impossible to understand Wal-Mart without peeking into the febrile brain of its charismatic patriarch.

Born in 1918 in Kingfisher, Oklahoma, Sam Walton was reared in a functional, if not a happy, family. His father, Thomas Gibson Walton, was an entrepreneur whose ventures in farming, insurance, and banking were never wildly successful. Whether this was the result of austere economic times or lack of business sense is not clear; it was hard to tell one from the other in Dust Bowl Oklahoma. Walton's mother, Nan, was an intelligent woman with ambitions for college that were shelved upon her marriage. By all accounts, it was her thwarted dream that motivated her eldest son. In search of better luck, Thomas Walton moved his family from Oklahoma into small Missouri towns like Shelbina and Marshall.

The roaring twenties were about as kind to Missouri as the nineties tech boom was to Youngstown, Ohio. The end of World War I had closed Europe's market to American farmers, and huge surpluses resulted. Prices fell, hard. Then the stock market crashed. As if on cue, the soil of Oklahoma, Nebraska, the Dakotas, and western Missouri dried up, and the dust storms forced farmers off their lands. These states were the origin of the massive westward exodus famously chronicled in the ballads of Woody Guthrie, the photographs of Dorothea Lange, and the novels of John Steinbeck.

In Shelby County, where the Waltons lived in the town of Shelbina, agriculture had peaked nearly thirty years earlier, and so had the population. With farm consolidation and the absence of other industries, the county's economy faltered. While FDR's New Deal assisted struggling farmers via the Agricultural Adjustment Administration, Shelby County was overlooked because, as bad off as it was, it wasn't as desperately dry as Kansas or the Dakotas.

During the worst of these Dust Bowl years, Thomas Walton worked for his half brother's firm, Walton Mortgage Co., an agent for the Metropolitan Life Insurance Company. He was, essentially, a repo man: driving far into the devastated Missouri countryside, he informed hardworking farm families that the way of life they'd known for generations was at an end. Traveling with his father, a young Mr. Sam got a vivid glimpse of extreme rural poverty. Bud Walton would later comment that witnessing this destitution made a profound impression on his brother: the drawn faces of the farm wives, the rags the children wore, the look in the eyes of the farmers when Walton Senior would take possession of their meager belongings. These were images that, it seems, never left Sam Walton's consciousness.

In the ensuing years, however, this childhood experience would take on a tinge of epiphany akin to Scarlett O'Hara's turnip-handed declaration to never go hungry again. Walton denied it was ever so pat, though that didn't stop business writers and other custodians of his legend from calling it a turning point. In *The Wal-Mart Decade,* Robert Slater gushes, "He had seen poverty firsthand as a child, and it became a personal crusade to lift the standard of living of those most in need of such lifting."[5]

Hagiographers and corporate teenyboppers would consider blasphemous the suggestion that Walton's experience watching farm foreclosures, rather than making him empathetic to the plight of the impoverished, hardened him. As father and son drove back from Shelbina after a hard day of evictions, which conversation was more likely?

"You know son, what enables your father to do this miserable work is his cold reptilian blood."

Or: "It's sad, son, what's going on, but these people can't afford to live here anymore. You see, in the free enterprise system . . ."

Could it be possible that the scenes of failure he witnessed struck Walton as an unfortunate, but entirely inevitable, part of a capitalistic system?

Getting hipped to social Darwinism at an early age could illuminate something new about Walton. Perhaps, during those trips to dying Dust Bowl farms, Walton identified with the behemoth rather than the little guy, even though he was the little guy. Perhaps there was something shameful in being the little guy.

MOST VERSATILE BOY

Big guys start little, though, and Sam Walton's first business was a joint venture with the family cow: selling milk to neighbors. He later abandoned Bessie and sold magazine subscriptions, delivered newspapers, and performed odd jobs around town. When Sam was fifteen, the Waltons moved from Shelbina to Columbia, home to the University of Missouri and a few smaller private colleges. At Hickman High School, Walton was voted president of the student body. At a less-than-commanding five-foot-nine, he managed to letter in both football and basketball, coming off the bench to play guard for the undefeated state championship hoops team.

Walton graduated from high school in 1936, having been awarded a yearbook designation quite suited for a future general merchandiser: "Most Versatile Boy." He stayed in Columbia to attend the University of Missouri, where he majored in economics and minored in exhaustion. Walton recalled his college years as the busiest in his life. He was involved in the campus Christian organization, was president of the student body, and was also part of the elite ROTC honor society, Scabbard and Blade. Meanwhile he was acing classes, juggling several jobs, and organizing the delivery of newspapers for the *Columbia Missourian*. He used the money he made, $4,000 to $5,000 a year, to cover his room, board, and fraternity dues. It's an astonishing sum: according to census figures, only 1.6 percent of all Missourians earned as much as $3,000 to $4,999 in those years.[6]

While Walton's hustle seems, at least in hindsight, to have been divinely appointed, there was, according to him, no otherworldly calling that led him to retail. Had he been able to afford the tony Wharton Business School, he would probably have gone on to be a revolutionary insurance broker (consider yourself lucky, Hartford!). But he couldn't afford it, and, really, he wasn't too interested. As he put it, "I got into retailing because I was tired and I wanted a real job."

While awaiting army orders during World War II, Sam Walton met Helen Robson at a bowling alley outside Tulsa in 1942. With a degree in finance from the University of Oklahoma, Helen worked in her father's law office in nearby Claremore. Three days after receiving his bachelor's degree, Sam Walton had headed north to Des Moines and the J. C. Penney management-training program, where he spent eighteen months falling in love with an industry he would change forever. Walton had just left the program when he met Helen, and was working in a gunpowder factory outside Tulsa. Their courtship was quick and intense, sparked by Sam's effective, if not terribly original line, "Don't I know you from somewhere?"* They were married on Valentine's Day, 1943.

Helen's father was Leland Stanford Robson, a well-established, self-made lawyer and rancher. Many of his unusual financial practices, like incorporating family members into a business partnership, with each member an equal partner, were quickly adopted by the young Waltons. (This is one reason Helen and her four children still rank high in the list of the Forbes 400 richest Americans.)

Leland Robson believed in his new son-in-law, and fronted funds for the young man's business ventures. Helen, too, supported Walton's

---

*Several biographers have remarked on the pickle that ensued when one of Walton's previous girlfriends, a cashier from Penney's, tracked him down in Oklahoma. Apparently, the two had been courting despite the company's policy against such relationships. While Sam thought he'd ended the affair, the woman was under a different impression. Perhaps this was the reason Walton later adopted Penney's same policy against in-store dalliances.

earliest stabs at retail: she underwrote several major loans for his enterprises, using her share in her father's estate, including a guarantee that later allowed Walton to take ownership of the Bank of Bentonville. This would enable him to finance his first Wal-Mart stores. The Walton Empire, then, could be said to have sprung from Helen Robson's pocketbook.

Immediately after being released from the army, Walton looked into the possibility of setting up a department store in St. Louis with an old college buddy. When he floated the idea to Helen, she quickly set down a two-point fatwa: because of her family's bad experience with outside partners, there would be none from outside the Robson-Walton clan; and, more significant, she would not live in a big city. Her population cap was 10,000.

This single decision, based on his wife's personal proclivity, forced Sam Walton into the demographic boonies. However unwittingly, Helen's decree would forever change the course of retailing, as it forced her husband, and those he employed, to think differently.

SAMMY'S NEW TOYS

So we arrive in Newport, Arkansas; it's 1950 and Sam Walton is pushing a lot of panties. But after losing his lease, Walton leaves Newport to try his luck in another small Ozark town. Bentonville was nestled in the state's northwest corner, with a population of only 3,000. Like Newport, it was not a pretty demographic: the population was half the size of Newport, and the town was already fitted with two five-and-dimes. But "Walton's 5¢ and 10¢"—now a Wal-Mart museum and one of the few things still open on Bentonville's town square—was the staging ground for more innovations. Most of these ideas were pinched from other retailers, as Walton would later admit, but he was like that kid in class who always had the latest toy a good month before anyone had even heard of it. And one of the first big toys was a concept called "self-service."

Like remote controls, touch-tone phones, or ATMs, self-service has become so common that it is hard to imagine stores operating any other way. But in a small Arkansas town in the early 1950s it was indeed a radical notion. In those days, stores required clerks to wait on customers, plucking the desired merchandise off shelves from behind long counters. Even small stores could require several registers. Perhaps the best contemporary analog is the remaining big-city department stores, with their separate counters for jewelry, cosmetics, perfume, handbags, sunglasses, men's accessories, and so on.

Thanks to the growing prominence of national brands and, later, television advertising, consumers became more educated about what they were after and less in need of hand-holding from clerks. But when Walton first read about two Ben Franklins in Minnesota that had gone to self-service, the idea of a customer serving herself was almost laughable. Walton, however, was intrigued and hopped a bus to make the 600-mile journey north. Liking what he saw—namely, a way to free up badly needed space for more goods while reducing the number of clerks—he swiftly deployed self-service in his Bentonville shop. It worked. By the mid-fifties, Walton had built up his Bentonville operation and was pressing on to open more Ben Franklin stores in Little Rock, Siloam Springs, and Fayetteville. The postwar economy was blowing up and the demand for goods had never been greater. Walton could sense the tide was turning. The little five-and-dimes would not be able to meet the demand for much longer.

Against the advice of his Air Force pilot brother, in 1957 Sam Walton purchased a beater of an Air Coupe for less than $2,000 and learned to fly. Being compulsively determined, and not a very good pilot, Walton was involved in more than a few close calls. He once tried taking off in three inches of snow on an unplowed runway. Staff at the Fayetteville airport would later find his plane plopped down, nose-first, in the middle of the runway. When air traffic controllers warned him he was flying too low, he merely switched off his radio, like it was a minor irritant.

From the air Walton could see how a community was growing and could pinpoint the logical spot for another store. Where other chains worked with market surveys and demographic data, Walton relied on little more than his own eyes. Sometimes it was only a matter of touching down, finding the property owner, and striking a deal. By the early sixties, Walton was operating seventeen stores in Arkansas and Kansas, and was the second-largest Ben Franklin operator in America. But he knew change was coming, even to the small towns he served. All over the country, the center of retail was moving away from the downtown nexus, to what were then called "family centers," where land was cheaper and parking plentiful.

Nineteen sixty-two would prove historic for retailing. That was the year the giants were born. In Michigan, S. S. Kresge opened a chain of discount stores called Kmart. The Minneapolis-based Dayton Hudson company debuted its own version, called Target. New York–based Woolworth's, whose lunch counters were hosting some of the earliest civil rights showdowns, introduced Woolco. And in Argentina, France's Carrefour opened a colossal oddity, a hybrid store of the sort America would not see for another two decades. It combined groceries with general merchandise and was called a "hypermarket," progenitor of the Wal-Mart Supercenter.

That same year, on July 2, without the backing of any established corporation, Sam Walton opened Wal-Mart Discount City in Rogers, Arkansas.

DISSED AND DISMISSED

No triumph-over-adversity narrative would be complete, or believable, without the hero's suffering a string of setbacks and humiliations. For Walton, the first blow was losing the lease on his hard-earned, successful Newport store because in the rush to establish himself he proved the slightest bit negligent (he forgot to read the fine print of his contract). Another came while he was traveling around the country, studying regional operators who were quietly pioneering the trade of discounting. Walton sniffed around other chains now consigned to the dustbin of discount history: Spartan, Mammoth Mart, Fed-Mart,* Two Guys from Harrison, and many others.

While most of these retailers were congenial, Herb Gibson was not. In the late fifties, the native Arkansan sat atop a 500-store, Texas-based chain that seemed poised to become the next Kmart. When Walton flew to Houston to meet with him, Gibson kept Walton waiting in his office for five hours. Finally, Walton was ushered into Gibson's office.

"Do you have one hundred thousand dollars?" Gibson asked Walton.

"No."

"Well, we buy in carload lots. Takes a lot of money to do that."

"But I—"

"You're not fixed to do business with us. Good-bye."[7]

But Walton's most famous rejection came when he went before

---

*Fed-Mart didn't exactly die. Its legendary founder, Sol Price, is generally considered the auteur of today's discount clubs. Walton modeled his Sam's Clubs after Price's Fed-Marts, so named as they originally catered only to government workers. Price was also the mentor of Jim Sinegal, who went on to establish Costco in the mid-1990s.

the Butler Brothers board of directors in the winter of 1962, just a few months after opening his first Wal-Mart on his own coin. At the company's Chicago headquarters, Walton told a roomful of experienced metropolitan retailers something they didn't want to hear, especially not from some backwoods franchisee: the day of the five-and-dime had passed. He had seen the future and its name was discounting. "Let me be your guinea pig," Walton begged after explaining the concept of Wal-Mart.

Even if he would have liked to cut them out of the supply game, Walton still thought Butler Brothers was his best, perhaps his only, option for what he rightly perceived as the inevitable move into discounting. Nearly all his five-and-dimes were financed on the fly, distinct partnerships between himself and his brother Bud, his father, Helen's two brothers, even his children. It was an exhausting process he yearned to be free from. And Butler Brothers was the ticket, an infrastructure for purchasing and distribution, not to mention start-up capital. Walton explained that with discounting, the margins would have to be reduced by at least half, perhaps more. But as much as he tried to make the board see how the company would make it up (and more) in volume, it was not to be. Butler Brothers said no.

As difficult as the rebuff must have been, the true movie moment came six months later, just as the first Wal-Mart, in Rogers, Arkansas, opened its doors. Like a cabal of crusty college deans putting the kibosh on an unruly fraternity, a flying column of Butler Brothers suits stormed into Wal-Mart and tersely demanded that Walton not "open any more of these Wal-Mart stores." This seemed only to energize Walton; if he'd obeyed, the landscape of suburban America might look very different than it does today. The first stores may have looked cracker-box, clothes hanging from pipes and laid out on folding tables, but in Rogers, Walton had all the ingredients. Even if, when lines grew long, cigar boxes doubled as cash registers, the limited but low-priced merchandise still flew out of the store. Walton knew his small-town demographic had more game than anyone had yet realized. They were shoppers hungry to be served stuff cheap, and Walton was ready to fill that gap.

Walton began cracking the whip. When his early teams of executives would break for home at 5:30 P.M., they'd invariably meet their boss as he bounded up the stairs and called an impromptu meeting that went on for two hours. Walton was known to show up in the home office as early as three or four in the morning. Despite the pleading of his wife, he insisted that it set a bad example to take Saturday off when people in the stores didn't enjoy the same privilege. While seemingly noble, this was also a way to ensure his workaholism became the normative standard for Bentonville execs.

Walton's carefully cultivated humility, which later became his company's ethos, would divert attention from the way employees were treated, both in terms of the wages they earned and the health-insurance plans they pined for but could not afford. It was as if his personal thrift was positioned as a fair trade-off for his almost diabolical business practices. Walton was a convincing down-home, aw-shucks guy; but at the end of the day, the stores were still called Wal-Mart.

A STINKING SUCCESS

The first Wal-Mart Discount Cities of the 1960s were no one's model of corporate efficiency. They were barely even stores. In fact, some of the company's greatest folklore comes from this period of low-roofed, non-air-conditioned buildings, where merchandise was often dumped onto foldout tables. Some shirts here, shoes there, but the low prices and a lack of competitors made Wal-Mart Discount Cities a hit nonetheless.

Easily the most famous Wal-Mart campfire story has former CEO David Glass, then a financial officer at a Missouri-based drugstore chain, witnessing the opening of the second Wal-Mart in Harrison, Arkansas. As part of the opening-day festivities Sam had hired donkeys for the kids to ride and stacked truckloads of watermelons outside the entrance. The sweltering August day grew so hot that the fruit began to pop, and the donkeys began to plop. Glass, whom Walton was then trying to woo into his flock, was deeply underwhelmed.

"It was the worst retail store I had ever seen," he'd later recall.[8] Glass even went so far as to suggest that maybe his future boss might want to consider another line of work.*

Despite the inauspicious beginning, Walton was optimistic. He had glimpsed the glories of Kmart and other larger competitors and understood that his stores' somewhat random product mix would need to be improved, and that key to this was distribution. One of the main reasons Wal-Mart's supply chain would ultimately become so efficient was that it had to. Recall Helen Walton's decree that she wouldn't live in a town larger than 10,000. This kept Walton far from big competition and allowed him to corner what would become a very important yet neglected market: rural and suburban families. (Had Helen held too firmly to her conviction, she'd have had to move out of her Bentonville home when Wal-Mart's growth increased the town's population to over 10,000. In 2004, the population of Bentonville was nearing 20,000.)

---

*As payback for imparting this anecdote to a magazine, Glass was forced to ride around the Harrison store parking lot on a donkey. In fact, donkeys have since become part of the Wal-Mart culture, and Lee Scott, Tom Coughlin, and retired executive Don Soderquist all rode them around the parking lot of the Rogers store to mark Wal-Mart's fortieth anniversary in 2002.

A MOST MODEST TITAN

Why Wal-Mart became Wal-Mart and not one of thousands of other short-lived retail outfits with similar models has a lot to do with Sam Walton, of course, but it also has to do with the people he surrounded himself with, and his willingness to let them do their jobs. However, if Walton was single-handedly responsible for one thing, it was creating the company's corporate culture, one that remains largely intact despite the company's legal and public relations troubles. Walton could rip off retailing ideas like self-service and models like the wholesale club, but he couldn't borrow a knack for motivating people or the ability to remember that the husband of a minimum-wage clerk in a store he hadn't visited in a year was in the hospital. As the company grew, so did Walton's mystique. His honed humility served, ironically, to elevate him to an almost godlike status among his employees. Later, Walton would become the smiley face on what many would come to see as a mean company.

Despite the "aw-shucks" attitude, there's reason to believe Walton played a hand in the construction of his myth. Take the ten-foot rule, an edict he spread like a service industry sacrament. In his routine, often unannounced, store visits, Walton would round up all the hourly associates and have them pledge aloud that if they should come within ten feet of a customer they'd smile and ask, "How can I help you?" They were then to close the pledge by saying: "So help me Sam." Walton could get away with demanding this sort of religious devotion—and instead of seeming arrogant, he came off as disarming and inspirational.

Examples of Walton's modesty are legion, and it's this modesty that gives a demonized company the institutionalized moral capital it so desperately needs. In 1985, when Walton topped the Forbes 400 as the world's richest man, he was driving a Ford pickup outfitted with cages for his slobbering hounds. He still lived with his wife, in the same small town, in the same nice but not princely home. And for a rich guy, he often had no money on him. Many of his executives recall how he was always bumming change for a pay phone or to buy a can of Coke. He chastised his staff for their high-end taste in cars, as it was not in keeping with the appearance of "just folks" humility.[9] He got his monthly haircut at the town barber for all of five dollars, and he didn't tip. At his own headquarters in Bentonville, he did not reserve a parking space for himself. His home phone number remained in the book until the day he died. And Sam Walton was also a Wal-Mart shopper (one of his attorneys noted that his shoes likely cost more than Walton's entire wardrobe).

So Walton drove a pickup truck, shot quail, and probably spent more time studying Kmart than Kmart's own executives, and as a result he embodied a peculiarly American paradigm that still endures in Bentonville to this day. He was a self-made, rock-'em-sock-'em capitalist cowboy in an industry devoted to peddling every fathomable consumer good, and yet he remained puritanically frugal in his personal and corporate expenditures.

Even Walton's leisure pursuits reflected a curious class split. On the one hand, he would play a genteel game of tennis—in charity tournaments, no less—while, on the other, he was far more fond of hunting quail, something he flew all over the country to do. When entering his stores he wore his "Sam" name tag like any other associate. Then, as now, Wal-Mart had no executive dining rooms or lavatories. Walton even refused to purchase a corporate jet because he believed it offered the impression of decadence. Leading by example, Walton created this unique corporate culture in which thrift was both a virtue and an imperative. It was a binary that was not lost on those visitors to Bentonville who came from the world beyond retailing. In the wake of the 1987 stock-market crash, former National Securities Association chairman John Bachmann addressed Walton and other executives at a Saturday-morning meeting. After a brief explanation of the crash, Bachmann found that talk quickly returned to the minutiae of the stores. "Here was a man who lost a billion dollars in one afternoon on the stock market spending more time talking about how one of his stores sold $700 worth of crepe paper," he recalled in astonishment.[10]

That these stories still resonate with Wal-Mart employees and customers has less to do with Walton's cornpone populism than with how he seemed to wrestle with a larger conflict. While doing everything in his power to make himself a success, he had zero interest in what this success might afford him. In fact, he held most of the trappings of success in contempt.

Even the way he used language was an effort to remove his ego from the business. In his column in the company newsletter, *Wal-Mart World,* Walton would often refer to "these Wal-Mart stores" or "our Wal-Mart stores" or "these doggone Wal-Marts," as though the business were not the culmination of his life's work, a venture he'd borrowed and begged to achieve. Rather, it rendered "Wal-Mart" a fickle crop to which he and his army of associates were mysteriously bound.

THE PEOPLE'S BILLIONAIRE

In April of 1992, George H. W. Bush took time off the campaign trail to visit the home state of his challenger, Bill Clinton. Before hundreds of tearful Wal-Mart associates, he awarded Sam Walton the

Presidential Medal of Freedom. Three weeks later, at age seventy-four, Walton died of bone cancer. In his final months Walton had lain on a makeshift bed inside his Bentonville office and received chemotherapy treatment. Even when hospitalized, he continued to work, communicating with the aid of a dry-erase board and an anti-gravity pen. One of his last visitors was a store manager, with whom he discussed the week's sales.

Wal-Mart has grown by a factor of five since Walton's death. It has begun operations in eight more countries on three more continents. At home the company has exhausted much of its rural base, while the bitch goddess of growth forces it into hostile turf. And not just into urban markets where the remaining vestiges of labor-union power still linger, but into upscale suburbs and exurbs that already enjoy an abundance of retail options. With the added scrutiny of being the world's largest . . . well, you name it, issues that began to surface toward the end of Walton's reign were destined to boil over big-time as the fire got hotter. That one man could have managed it all is a fallacy. Sam Walton didn't crawl out of a coal mine or plop from the fire escape of a dirty brick tenement. He never took shrapnel on Omaha Beach, or planted a flag on a bombed-out island in the Pacific theater. The hard-knocks road from poverty to prosperity, the vanquishing of demons both personal and political that is the preferred narrative for CEOs and *Oprah* guests alike is often confused with Walton's life story, but they're not cut from the same cloth. True, economic necessity kept the family moving, and once, according to Walton, his father hawked his wristwatch for a hog. But it was a Walton who was collecting the last belongings of a farm family during the Dust Bowl, and not the other way around.

Thinking about the Walton legend, it's hard to believe his company would become one of the most divisive, most reviled—and, simultaneously, the most profitable and admired—institutions of our time. Walton's little five-and-dime has become a company whose vaguest of public pronouncements trigger *New York Times* editorials.[11] It's become something of a cliché within circles of Wal-Mart associates and observers to wax nostalgic, if not messianic, about how everything would be different if Sam were still alive.

But as former *Wall Street Journal* reporter Bob Ortega detailed in his book *In Sam We Trust,* Walton was no saint. He broke labor laws to keep workers from joining unions; he violated minimum-wage laws when he could get away with it; and though he encouraged debate among his executives, when push came to shove he was not shy about slamming his fist down. As former senior executive Don Soderquist recalled him saying, "By golly, I still own most of the stock in this company and this is the way we're going to do it."[12]

Walton somehow synthesized two warring angels of American nature: a hunger for success, and a puritanical revulsion for the accoutrements of that very same success. Walton built an empire on selling America stuff, but he never betrayed any affection for the stuff, beyond the many ways it might be stacked or positioned to "blow out the store." He even expressed fear that his progeny would become part of the idle rich, a class he "never had much use for."[13]

Perhaps it was because he was born into the mainstream, or because his heart and mind could be found in the store aisles where his customers shopped for stuff more than status, but Walton never came off as a phony. In the decades since his death, none of the dirt that has surfaced about him has managed to tarnish his reputation, even while his company has suffered more hits on a wider variety of fronts than any American business in history.

In many ways Sam Walton is the billionaire we all secretly want to be: a man whose authentic self could never be altered by any amount of wealth or power. The myth of "Mr. Sam" is not about low margins or stickin' it to the status quo of American business. It's not about panties, or even panty-ology. It's all about how you can be the richest man in America and never sell out. Walton was less a genius, though, than a monomaniac in the right place at the right time, a man whose paradoxical relationship to wealth and power is in sync with the nation's own puritan-derived ambivalence.

The more time that has elapsed since his death, the more Wal-Mart seems to need Sam Walton—to provide a public face more genuine than executives who speak only in well-rehearsed media talking points; to mitigate fears that its size and power are turning Bentonville into a Death Star and the country at large into its serfs; most of all, Wal-Mart needs Sam Walton to help sort out the monster he created. And in the absence of the man, they'll settle for his ghost.

THREE

THE GROWTH MACHINE

Wal-Mart's folkloric status as a straight-out-of-nowhere success story is inextricably linked with the cult that surrounds the person of Sam Walton. Since his death in 1992, the Oklahoma-born wunderkind has gone from company front man to a deity unlike any the corporate world has known. As if he were the Castro of the big-box set (if Castro were a raging capitalist), Mr. Sam's sayings and likeness adorn company headquarters and outposts. Executives and flacks endlessly recycle his anecdotes and "rules" as if company history ceased upon his death.

For its first thirty years, Wal-Mart never had to worry much about having a corporate personality. But since Walton's death, the way the company is perceived, by everyone from the media to its own customers, has undergone a radical and unflattering transformation: from scrap-happy underdog to global despot. Overseas sweatshops, systemic gender discrimination, and health insurance priced beyond employees' paltry wages are issues that never quite disappear. Wal-Mart battles a medley of salvos while continuing to grow at a double-digit rate. Its only defense, outside of its size and power, is its culture, the cult of Sam.

CHAMPION OF CHEAP

Sam Walton built his empire on a belief that rural America could generate more business than anyone in the corporate world was recognizing. This vision, combined with a zealot's dedication to low overhead, undercutting the competition through lower profit margins and higher sales volumes, investment in technology, and aggressive growth, blazed a trail for an imperial corporation that now operates in nine countries.

As Sears, Kmart, and J. C. Penney operated like nomads, following their flock of customers from city to suburb, Wal-Mart quietly stuck to the small towns. While American cities were sent reeling in the 1970s by white flight, deindustrialization, and a lousy economy, it was a great time for the boonies. Suburbs were exploding with new development and fast-rising populations. Between 1972 and 1977 retail sales in rural areas grew at nearly twice the rate of urban markets. And Wal-Mart was there to lap it up, as stores multiplied like gremlins at a water park.

In its forty-year history, Wal-Mart has amassed a jaw-dropping trophy rack of titles, including "world's largest corporation," edging out stellar corporate citizen ExxonMobil for the top spot in 2002,

2003, and 2004 Fortune 500 rankings. With Kmart (until recently its closest rival) now in bankruptcy, the path is clear to ever greater domination.

Despite the company's unbelievable wealth, the corporate culture remains largely the same as the one Walton so skillfully crafted while he was alive. Its competing tenets are egalitarianism, low-key anti-individualism, and an almost missionary purpose to serve something larger than oneself. As the famous, if not original, company cheer asks and answers: "Who's number one? Who's number one? The customer, always."

Sam Walton branded his chain as a purveyor of no frills, "just folks" populism and low prices. It's simple and easy. Its Rollback Smiley mascot is so bland it makes *The Family Circus* look subversive (except, perhaps, when Smiley is dressed up like Zorro). But the Wal-Mart ethos is also rooted in being the champion of cheap. As the dueling slogans state: "Always the Low Price" and "We Sell for Less." The implication is clear: it's as if all other stores are conspiring against the customer, gleefully rubbing their hands together and hoping the innocent shopper will overpay for her mashed potato mix. Evil forces are amassing against us, Wal-Mart's advertising seems to insinuate, and the only safe haven is in the local Wal-Mart.

With this idea now firmly embedded in the collective cost-conscience of a nation, Wal-Mart is free, at times, to *not* sell for less and not suffer loss of customers. In the mid-nineties, the chain was called out by Target and other competitors for its misleading newspaper circulars and in-store price comparison placards. Retailers consistently charged that Wal-Mart inflated its competitors' prices and kept the promos running long after those competitors had reduced them to combat the smear. For this tactic, the Better Business Bureau's advertising review panel ruled against Wal-Mart in a case regarding its slogan; in a rare act of (forced) contrition, Wal-Mart changed "Always the Low Price, Always" to the more modest "Always Low Prices."[1]

Years of this Wal-Marketing has solidified the perception that all of Wal-Mart's prices are the lowest. According to former Wal-Mart executive Michael Bergdahl, it simply isn't true.

"Shopping cart comparisons will prove Wal-Mart's prices are not the lowest on all items," Bergdahl wrote in his 2004 book *What I Learned from Sam Walton.* "There is, however, a perception in the mind of the consumer that they are. This perception has been strategically planted there by targeted advertising and marketing messages focused on Wal-Mart's 'everyday low prices' campaign. Consumers begin to believe that Wal-Mart has the lowest prices on everything so they stop doing comparison shopping."[2]

Another ex Wal-Mart man, store manager Jon Lehman, described to PBS's *Frontline* in 2004 a similar method by which the company manipulates its low-price appeal for maximum gain. By placing displays of high margin electronics in strategic sales floor locations, managers lure customers intrigued by the "opening price point" display deeper into the store, where the rest of the product category is on display. There, prices are less likely to be the lowest, but a significant number of customers will notice that for an additional five or ten dollars they can trade up for a better model, one on which Wal-Mart will profit significantly more. Get a customer to do that a few times each visit, and suddenly you're *Fortune*'s most admired company.

"Once you walk past that opening price point," Lehman told *Frontline,* "they got you because you've already formed the perception that everything in that department is the lowest price in town."[3]

FOOD AND BEYOND

From the opening of the first Supercenter in Washington, Missouri, in 1988, it took Wal-Mart only twelve years to claim the mantle of world's largest grocery store. The road it traveled to get there is littered with the stinking corpses of countless regional chains and independent groceries. If Wal-Mart has come to seem less like a choice than an inevitability, there's a good reason for it: Wal-Mart is going to become an inevitability. Beginning in the mid-nineties, grocery stores and general retailers, much like TV networks and newspapers, began a feeding frenzy of buyouts and mergers that has yet to abate. The highlight—or lowlight, depending on your point of view—of this frenzy was the merger, in November 2004, of Sears and Kmart. Wal-Mart's venture into the grocery game, which got off to a wobbly start in the late 1980s, was really rolling by the mid 1990s. Until then the grocery business was composed of regional powers, with a small vanguard of national players like Safeway and Kroger. Winn-Dixie and Piggly Wiggly took much of the South; A&P, Shoprite, and Shaws serviced the Northeast; Ralph's and Safeway took care of the West Coast, Fred Meijer the Midwest, and Fred Meyer the Northwest. Other chains blanketed smaller subregions.

One of the consequences of regional consolidation in the 1980s was a spike in food prices, something that couldn't have proved more fortuitous for Wal-Mart, because it enabled the burgeoning leviathan to undercut its competitors on price while simultaneously learning the grocery business. By the mid-nineties it had become quite clear that Wal-Mart's food venture wasn't going to fail, as so many had predicted, and hoped. In fact, Supercenters, with their combo retail/grocery stores, were becoming Wal-Mart's number-one growth vehicle, finally outpacing the original Wal-Mart variety store in 2001.

The company's buying clout had a spillover effect for smaller chains that couldn't afford to order at the volume of Wal-Mart and the national chains. In an effort to prepare for the frenzy, big fish ate smaller fish in prolonged scenes of cannibalization. In the span of two years, the grocery chain Albertsons acquired 179 American Stores; the Dutch Royal Ahold chain picked up Giant Food in the South and Stop & Shop in the Northeast, while Safeway swallowed Vons and Dominick's in California. Small drugstores were also gobbled up as the national trend toward managed health care forced pharmacies to bulk up in order to negotiate with insurers.

As many would learn the hard way, mergers were not the most effective means of loosening Wal-Mart's death grip on the market. While these mergers increased a company's buying power, they also required complex systems integration and management restructuring, which was a suck on time and capital. Both Safeway and Albertsons would find themselves bogged down in sorting out their mergers while Wal-Mart pushed further into their markets. And then there were the variety-store retailers who went belly up. One could fashion a Maya Lin–type monument with the names of the dead: Woolworth's,* Caldor, Bradlees, Ames, E. J. Korvette, McCrory, Jamesway, Gibson's, and on and on. Between 1993 and 2003, twenty-nine chains filed for bankruptcy; in all but four cases, the companies cited competition from Wal-Mart as the reason.[4]

Wal-Mart's domestic growth has been largely organic, merger-free. This is not the case in its International Division, where, because of the high cost of real estate and the implausibility of re-creating its distribution system in a foreign market, Wal-Mart has grown almost entirely through acquisitions. The company kicked off Wal-Mart

---

*Though Woolworth's was once the iconic American dime store, it died a quiet death in the early nineties. However, it continues to operate in the UK.

Canada by snatching one-hundred-plus stores from the Woolworth-owned Woolco chain; in Mexico, Wal-Mart bought up Cifra; in Brazil it was Lojas Americanas; in Germany, Wertkauf became Wal-Mart property; South Korea's Makro, Britain's ASDA, and Japan's Seiyu were also brought into the Walton fold.

Though Wal-Mart vehemently denies that it is responsible for the decline of small businesses, there is little doubt that grocery stores, at the very least, are victims: for every Supercenter that opens, two grocery stores go under. In the process, Wal-Mart's presence in the market is quickly turning an industry that once had room for dozens and dozens of owner-operators into an oligopoly unlike any the world has ever seen.

THE CULTURE OF THRIFT

From regional vice presidents taking in hundreds of thousands a year to cashiers barely making ends meet, everyone is an "associate." When people make mistakes, they're not cited or written up, but "coached." Wal-Mart is not antiunion, it's "pro-associate." The company's "open door policy" allows anyone to state a problem or concern without fear of retaliation, thus, Wal-Mart claims, eliminating the need for union representation.

It's not just the language that gave birth to corporate collectivism. The perks the company offers its employees—profit sharing and discounted stock options—have certainly made some of the company's longtime associates quite rich. Some cashiers who joined the company years ago and who stuck it out have retired as millionaires or with a sizable enough chunk of change to live comfortably in rural America.

"There's absolutely no limit," Walton writes in his autobiography, "to what plain, ordinary working people can accomplish if they're given the opportunity and the encouragement and the incentive to do their best." This could easily be a stump speech of bipartisan banality. And Walton was nothing if not a passionate campaigner for his company, his shareholders, and his ever-growing army of associates. While the tone of his speeches was never bitter or divisive, Wal-Mart's mythology plays into a cultural politics that grows increasingly so.

In *What's the Matter with Kansas?* author Thomas Frank explores the phenomenon of how working-class white Republicans began voting against their economic interests. This shift hinged upon the redefinition of class as something rooted not in economics or power relations but in cultural tastes. Leading purveyors of this mythology, like *New York Times* columnist David Brooks, have established blue-state liberals as effete, latte-slurping Volvo drivers who read the *New York Times* and get religious about terra-cotta. In flyover land, however, live the most salt-of-the-earth Americans, who drive pickups, chug Coors, shoot things, and are religious about religion: the Jesus kind.

Subtract the economics from class politics, Frank argues, and the conflict becomes purely cultural. Within such a context, multimillionaires like Bill O'Reilly and Rush Limbaugh can howl like pitchfork-bearing proles while living like pampered princes.[5] George W. Bush can pose as a man of the people despite a background of privilege that nepotized him into Yale and Harvard. And Wal-Mart CEO Lee Scott can posture with defiance about how proud he is that two-thirds of his store managers did *not* attend these same Ivy League schools but were forged in the aisles of Wal-Mart.

Sam Walton was sure to have dodged charges of partisanship like they were the clap (why alienate a customer?) but the essence of Wal-Mart culture hinges upon this shift of workers' seeing their interests linked to the same corporation that is paying them a wage they can't live on and benefits they seldom see, then packaging this contradiction as something worth cheering about. What's more, because Sam Walton is an irreplaceable figurehead, the company having so seamlessly integrated his charisma into its culture that "What would Sam do?" has become a question of retail theology as pervasive as those bumper stickers about that Jewish carpenter guy.

POWERFUL? US?

American corporations have a history of trying to de-emphasize both their size and their influence; such is the imperative in a democracy that checks—or is supposed to—the power of branches of government, churches, and other forms of institutional power. Utilizing illustrations of its hometown headquarters in advertising, or featuring a benevolent-looking founder's visage in propaganda are two popular ways of creating what author and academic Roland Marchand called the corporate soul.[6] Despite Wal-Mart's aversion to PR, the core of the company's corporate soul could be found in the persona of Sam Walton. However, upon his death, executives reasoned that it was foolhardy for any of them to try to fill his shoes as the public face of Wal-Mart. So as the company consolidated its power it simultaneously faced the challenge of denying that it was, well, powerful.

Wal-Mart manifests itself in three main forms: the traditional Wal-Mart retail store, which peddles everything from panties to Pennzoil and averages about 90,000 square feet; Sam's Club, a warehouse-club store where "members" pay an annual fee to receive deep discounts on dry goods and groceries; and Supercenters, the company's biggest growth vehicle, a combination retail and grocery store clocking in at 190,000 square feet—and these babies are opening at a rate of one every day.

One retail analyst has likened Wal-Mart's strategy to Mao Zedong's "Conquer the countryside, then take the cities."

If this sounds alarmist, consider Wal-Mart's Neighborhood Market, the prototype grocery store that is roughly the size of three 7-Elevens. In the first years of the new millennium, Wal-Mart has deployed the stores for greater market saturation in urban strongholds like Oklahoma City and Dallas. While zoning laws and real estate costs impede the development of most forms of Wal-Mart in larger metropolitan areas, the trim Neighborhood Market might squeeze into places a Supercenter could never dream of occupying.

Since its baptism by fire in the 1960s, not a decade has gone by when Wal-Mart hasn't debuted a new form of technology. Whether it's the largest satellite and computer systems outside of government, or the elaborate information-gathering software, the purpose is the same: reduce costs by stomping out inefficiencies, and do so by mastering information. Wal-Mart doesn't invent any of its technology. Rather, it's like the kid who manages to rig his new train set through the house and into the front yard on Christmas morning while everyone else is still snoring.

Throughout the late 1960s and early seventies, Wal-Mart's executives waged a battle to convince their cost-crazed boss to invest in a host of different technologies. It was no easy fight. But it wasn't because Walton had his head in the sand. Just as he had been prescient enough to see that the days of the dime store were numbered, he also realized early on that computers would be at the heart of retailing's future.

A few years earlier, Walton had enrolled in IBM's school for retailers at its Poughkeepsie headquarters, where he not only educated himself but also started to identify the talent he'd need to position his growing fleet of stores for major growth.

It was logistics men like Jack Shewmaker and Ron Mayer and Bob Thornton, guys Walton plucked from regional competitors, who agitated and conspired to turn the company into a vanguard of distribution. The first warehouses were built too small and too late. The first automated freestanding distribution center that went up in 1977 was bursting with shipments before a roof was on, before toilets worked. It soon became the site of several unsuccessful Teamster organizing drives, as workers were being pushed beyond their wherewithal.

But with newly recruited executives like David Glass, Mayer from Texas's Duckwall Stores, and Don Soderquist, formerly of Ben Franklin, Wal-Mart's distribution centers went from being the company's embarrassment to the jewel in its logistical crown.

The change had partially to do with Walton finally adding more floor space to his stores; but it also had to do with early investment in computer technology. One of the first concessions Shewmaker and Glass wrestled from their boss was a computer network. Though it's entirely unremarkable today, when eight-year-olds expect wireless connectivity like it was breakfast in the morning, in 1977 the move was nothing short of revolutionary. Run through private phone lines, the network hooked the company's five hundred stores, as well as its two distribution centers, to the home office in a continuous loop of information.

The nerve center was anchored by two IBM mainframe 370s housed in a 16,000-square-foot building in Bentonville. In addition to storing sales data, it also kept the payroll, bank deposits, personnel records, and warehouse inventory.

Throughout the eighties, Wal-Mart worked on bringing its biggest suppliers into the system that would later become the industry standard known as electronic data interchange (EDI). A system of computer networks transferring data packets over private networks, EDI automated the processes of ordering, tracking, and paying. What once took up to ten days was now carried out in two or three.[7] And there were other efficiencies, such as fewer data-entry clerks making fewer mistakes with fewer expensive complications. Today nearly all of Wal-Mart's suppliers are EDI compliant—though instead of using private lines and archaic modems, they now use the Internet.

Today, in blue vests once adorned by the phrase "Our People Make the Difference" but now begging "How May I Help You?" Wal-Mart cashiers plop items into smiley-face-emblazoned plastic bags. No need to ponder "paper or plastic?"; the question has been settled for you. When a bag gets filled with Wal-crap, a gentle tap to a carousel puts an empty bag right where it needs to be. Baggers at Wal-Mart? About as likely as a shop steward.

In days gone by, it was the cash register's "ka-ching" that heralded every sale; in the automated era, a brief "blip" speaks volumes—and speaks of volume. And it's a sound a Wal-Mart manager had better hear a lot: 475 times an hour, per cashier, to be exact.

"I like to keep mine loud so that I can hear what has been scanned," says Wal-Mart cashier Tina Krieg, who works in a southern-Illinois Supercenter. "You get very used to it, as well as all the other sounds: the pages, the Wal-Mart TV, the crying children, it all becomes something you begin to tune out easily."[8]

To the executives and technocrats who actually run the company,[9] though, each blip kicks off a dazzlingly complex exchange of information among stores, distribution centers, and suppliers. Shoppers never see it and probably couldn't care less if they did, but it's this continually flowing stream of information culled largely from the contents of shopping carts that has as much to do with Wal-Mart's supremacy as its everyday low prices do. In fact, one could hardly exist without the other.

OUT OF STOCK: OUT OF BUSINESS

We may always have Coke and Cap'n Crunch, but the age of mass merchandising is effectively over. One size does not fit all, if it ever did to begin with. Technology has let retailers go beyond supplying our basic staples, even beyond ethnic niche marketing. Seasons, holidays, weather, a store's proximity to a college, a beach, or a competitor: all factor into a complex merchandising calculus fueled by decades of data collection and analysis.

Wal-Mart's 3,551 U.S. stores (through 2004) may look the same, but their shoppers are different. Sam Walton said that the bigger the company grew, the more important it was for them to think small; it's only through technology that Wal-Mart can think at all.

Studied in business schools, copied by competitors, even retrofitted for hospitals and the military, Wal-Mart's supply line is the envy of many and the heart and soul of its operation. No matter how mighty its market share, how vast its stores' square footage or how measly its labor costs, if the right stuff can't get to the right shelf at the right time there's no reason for it to exist. A simple idea, sure. But it's an idea that becomes immensely complicated when 3,551 stores carry 100,000 items from 60,000 suppliers.

Also known as a distribution system, the supply line is the process by which products get from manufacturer to store shelf. In a high-volume, low-margin industry like discount retailing, the importance of an efficient distribution system can't be overstated. At its essence, retailing is about turning over inventory as quickly and as often as possible.

For example: say that in the course of a day, four different toddlers are pacified by the purchase of a $13.99 "Potty with Elmo" doll. After each transaction is complete, the most important thing for a retailer is to ensure that there are more Elmos to potty with. This means more than just going to a stockroom to fill up. Even if you're not quite the hulking monster that is Wal-Mart, retail requires a system of assuring that replacements for the four Elmos are in the process of being plucked from a warehouse and shipped back to the store. Because, as the old retailing mantra goes, "When you're out of stock, you're out of business."

SCAN THIS!

One day in 1974 a pack of Juicy Fruit gum was sold at a Marsh supermarket in Troy, Ohio. For the first time, no price was punched into the register; all that was needed was a quick scan of several small lines that comprised a language all its own. Now known universally as UPCs or barcodes, the little lines are stickered on our luggage, library books, and even wristbands on children in day-care facilities. Throughout the world an estimated five billion scans occur daily; if the codes and scanners were suddenly to mysteriously fail, it's not very far-fetched to say that the entire global economy would skid to a halt.[10]

Though they had been used for years in manufacturing, barcodes were a tough sell for retailing. Grocery stores balked at the idea throughout the seventies. It wasn't until discounters like Wal-Mart, Kmart, and Sears took the plunge in the early eighties that the black lines started exploding into every crevice of the economy. Less than a decade later, they'd become so unremarkable that the only one still surprised was President George H. W. Bush, whose barcode bewilderment on the '92 campaign trail helped fuel charges that he was out of touch with America.

After years of experimenting and working out kinks, Wal-Mart debuted its "point of sale" scanners in twenty-five stores in 1983.

With both barcodes and EDI, Wal-Mart had gotten into the game early. Once accomplished, rolling out the system was a veritable cakewalk. Competitors suddenly realizing they, too, must code or die were now years behind Wal-Mart, even if they were larger.[11] Wal-Mart was nearly two times more productive than its competitors in 1987, back when it had only 9 percent of the retail market.[12]

With the two systems in place, the next phase seemed almost logical, if not for its obscene price tag. Knowing all too well the culture of the company, a data processing manager named Glenn Habern brought an idea to Shewmaker, and the two quietly researched what would, by 1987, become the largest private satellite system in the world.

While Sears and Kmart twiddled their thumbs, Bentonville was using its satellite system to control the temperature and lights in each of its stores, keep a tally on stolen credit cards, and monitor its sales in real time. The system saved the company millions in long-distance phone calls; it reduced credit-card authorization time from a minute to seven seconds; it even let trucks beam their location every fifteen minutes so stores and distribution centers could know if they were running late or early.

The satellite system also gave birth to Wal-Mart TV, a network of four channels broadcasting on a dozen monitors in each of over 2,500 stores. Over a four-week period in 2004, its net audience among eighteen-to-forty-nine-year-olds exceeded that of Fox's hit *American Idol.**[13]

---

*Speaking of Fox, Wal-Mart TV gets its news from Rupert Murdoch's very own fair and balanced network (Fox). On election night 2004, Wal-Mart shoppers would be the first to learn Ohio had given the presidency to George W. Bush. This is not to suggest Wal-Mart TV is part of an ideological scheme. Wal-Mart TV not only advertises products in the store, but also generates revenue: a fifteen-to-thirty-second spot goes for between $30,000 and $300,000.

None of this would be possible without "the brain." Located in a former aluminum plant two miles from the Bentonville home office, the David Glass Technology Center houses an IT department estimated to employ a thousand people. It's also the home to the world's largest data library: a 460-terabyte teradata computer system, which the *New York Times* put in perspective by saying it contains more data than the entire Internet. The brain collects all sales information from the retail stores, Sam's Clubs, and Neighborhood Markets, as well as approximately 1,520 stores in nine other countries. Oh, and it all happens in near-real time. The sale of a clock radio in a Wal-Mart in Shenzhen, China, for example, is reported in Bentonville within the hour.

The data-collection system works to create what IT geeks call a "knowledge colony": a collection of historical sales data that, to pervert an environmentalist slogan, operates globally to sell locally. The data fuel a software program Wal-Mart started using in the early nineties called Retail Link, which catalogues every sale at every store. Initially named "Buyer Decision Software System," Retail Link features thousands of "traits" that paint a complex profile of every single Wal-Mart store. Traits include everything from a store's proximity to a beach, a university, or a retirement community to what type of breakfast food a community buys after a natural disaster. If a variable exists, chances are it's in the system.

Even before Retail Link was fully operational, Bentonville's buyers were using it every chance they could get. In the early nineties, when someone abandoned their computer for lunch, it was quickly jumped on by a merchandiser wanting to run numbers. The home office soon started adding more and more workstations to permit its people greater access to the system. An internal audit had revealed the company was saving $12,000 per query.[14]

Wal-Mart allows its suppliers to access the information in Retail Link, and it has proven a substantial boon to many suppliers, as it enables them to see all the data Wal-Mart sees: all the hundreds of details on how their products are performing. This, in turn, enables the suppliers to mine the data to better focus their marketing and merchandising practices. Forging this direct relationship is part of the reason why Benton County, Arkansas, has become one of the fastest-growing counties in America, home to hundreds of Wal-Mart suppliers, large global corporations who've made the inevitable migration to "service the account." The flip side to this, of course, is the Big Brother element. When a bright lamp is shined on even the prettiest face, slight flaws are revealed. And before long they are punished.

But having a lot of data doesn't mean anything by itself. It's what they're used for that's the key. Wal-Mart's cavernous teradata system contains two years of sales information. Sometimes those data get used in basic cross-marketing of the sort Amazon has made us all too familiar with. "Customers who bought the *Faces of Death* DVD box set also bought *Wildest Street Fights Vol. 1.*" Mainly, though, it mines for patterns that enable Wal-Mart to better understand its customers.

Some data-driven merchandising seems intuitive. For instance, it might follow that lots of heavy rain in Texas would prompt a demand for mops. But who'da thunk that men buying diapers after work on Fridays were also picking up six-packs of beer? Or that Floridians prepping for a hurricane had a penchant for strawberry Pop-Tarts?[15] In some cases, it's only a matter of getting the right items to the stores in time for the flood, hurricane, or whatever other misfortune that proves profitable for Wal-Mart.

In other situations (like the diapers and brew) the data contribute to in-store displays that put the two seemingly disparate items together in a display. This is called "affinity marketing." Another example includes displaying toys with snack food and DVDs. Toys are the attention-grabber, and because kids link snacks with movies, Wal-Mart can incite three distinct cries of "I want it!" within a tiny fraction of floor space.[16]

Sometimes data queries are sociological surveys unto themselves. Take roaches, the impermeable critters that dodge rolled-up magazines like a president ducks hardball questions. It's safe to say that no one really welcomes these intruders, but how their presence reflects one's sense of self can take on a regional cast. In the South, buying a bottle of clearly marked "Roach Spray" is hardly a big deal, but in Lutheran Minnesota, it's akin to flaunting a moral failure. When Wal-Mart's data triggered this epiphany, it was only a matter of talking to its supplier, who quickly retooled the packaging so as to "kill" the roach's likeness. Sales quickly shot up: good news for Wal-Mart, if less so for Minnesotan roaches.

Keeping close tabs on each store prevents what could otherwise prove laughable mistakes. For instance, a store in the predominantly African-American area of Decatur, Georgia, will shelve dark-skinned Barbies, and the music section will lean toward a PG-13 Snoop Dogg, while the largely white store only twenty miles away in Dunwoody peddles Garth Brooks albums.[17]

SPAMOUFLAGE AND RETAILTAINMENT

There are many reasons to camouflage Spam. To protect one's culinary reputation. To prevent shame when consuming. To make money. The latter reason is why Wal-Mart asked Hormel Foods to come up with a gimmick to get hunters, who spend lots of money in Wal-Mart's sporting-goods aisles, to buy more Spam. Hormel came up with "Spamouflage"—Spam in camouflaged cans. It burned off the shelves.

In addition to Spamouflage, Wal-Mart also engages in a practice it calls "retailtainment," a marketing term that encompasses a host of in-store activities designed less as cultural enrichment—though presented as such—and more as a means of keeping bodies inside a store for as long as possible. Retailtainment isn't just confined to celebrity events or in-store concerts; it can also come in the form of a product demonstration, an in-store cooking class, or even a coupon dispenser. Readers wishing to meet bestselling authors like Nicholas Sparks or Timothy LaHaye may suddenly realize they need trash-can liners (if their subconscious is in working order). Others may decide that the Hanson lads performing on Wal-Mart TV are quite the toe-tappers and pick up a copy of the trio's latest CD (which is sure to be stocked nearby).

The practice fits snugly within Wal-Mart's overall strategy of encouraging crossover shopping; that is the art of encouraging customers to veer from their destination—say, groceries—to buy goods in other parts of the store, goods they had no intention of buying, and perhaps had even told themselves before visiting the store they *wouldn't* buy.

An important element in this kind of marketing is tailoring goods to local tastes. Moving from the general to the specific is a risky strategy, but Wal-Mart can absorb the risks. In Louisiana Wal-Marts you can find "Cajun Crawtator" potato chips—chips that taste like fish—and Mardi Gras cakes, topped with a chain of Mardi Gras beads. (*Forbes* reported that Wal-Mart sold an average of $2,100 worth of the cake each week.[18])

Suppliers are pressured to create variations of their goods to suit local bents, as well. Using regional information from Retail Link,

Pennzoil, for example, has created fifty different variations of its oil specifically for Wal-Mart. Two years earlier, Pennzoil had only five. *Forbes* estimated that that number would be up to 200 in the next few years.[19]

Data mining is not unique to Wal-Mart. Nearly all major chain supermarkets have so-called "loyalty cards" as part of their efforts toward precision marketing. Wal-Mart rejects the cards because they're almost always tied to promotional sales, which are contrary to the idea of "everyday low prices."

Had Wal-Mart not made the decision to move forward on technology early on, its sales and its size would not have skyrocketed as they did in the 1980s. In that decade alone, Wal-Mart jumped from a regional chain of 276 to a national upstart with 1,528 stores. At the same time its sales catapulted from $1.2 to $26 billion.

And now that it's so firmly planted in the number-one spot, where competitors are forced to sell in its shadow and fill in its many niches, Wal-Mart shows no sign of complacency. As a sign in the lobby of the David Glass Technology Center reads: WE MUST BE INVENTING AND IMPLEMENTING FASTER THAN THE COMPETITION IS STEALING. Recently it has been among the first to comply with a global data synchronization standard called UCCnet: a universal product code to establish accurate information so retailers and manufacturers who might not speak the same tongue can share a common language when it comes to differentiating Twinkies from lightbulbs. This has already cut the time for entering new products into its system from two weeks to two days.[20] But that's a mere sideshow compared to the main event.

In June of 2003, Bentonville's chief information czar, Linda Dillman, informed Wal-Mart's one hundred biggest suppliers that they had eighteen months to comply with a high-tech overhaul on a scale unseen since the barcode debuted thirty years before. It's called radio frequency identification, or RFID, and, like most things Wal-Mart has deployed to its benefit, it's not entirely new. Originally developed by the military during the Second World War, RFID helped keep American fighter planes from shooting each other down in the confusion of battle. And anyone who has used SpeedPass or E-ZPass to breeze through what were once tiresome highway toll-booths is already familiar with RFID, even if the technology is a mystery. It's actually not too complicated: a high-frequency radio signal is picked up by a tag, which consists of a piece of copper wire serving as the antenna and a computer chip embedded with coded data. Active tags scan for radio signals and can have the capacity to have data written to them. More common are "passive" tags that are woken up by a signal the same way a solar-powered calculator is turned on by light.

Where barcodes require a direct line of sight in order to be scanned, RFID tags can be picked out almost anywhere. For Wal-Mart's purposes, the tags are used at key points on the supply route: a tag's data can be processed by a reader, and a software system called Middleware translates its numerical code into readable text, enabling retailers and suppliers to know where their stuff is at any given moment.

That RFID and Wal-Mart would end up in bed together shouldn't come as too big a surprise. In 1999 the company was one of several retailers and manufacturers that helped fund MIT's Auto ID Center, a not-for-profit institute established to help set standards for the technology. According to Linda Dillman, Wal-Mart started experimenting with RFID on its own in 2001 at a lab in Rogers, Arkansas, home of the first Wal-Mart.[21]

Wal-Mart's RFID announcement was a wake-up call for more than just its top hundred suppliers. When the company jumped in headfirst, competitors had little choice but to follow suit. Within months of its announcement Target, Home Depot, and Albertsons all announced RFID programs of their own. The Department of Defense also had its own mandate. RFID became a buzzword across multiple industries, but in retailing the big question had to do with another acronym: ROI (return on investment).

A few months after the decree, Wal-Mart invited suppliers to Bentonville for an informational summit to ease concerns and answer questions. Suppliers complying on time should not expect any increased business from Wal-Mart as a reward, attendees were told, and despite some technical difficulties the deadline would hold. As one executive attending the meeting recalled, "No one raised their hand and said, 'Excuse me?'"[22]

Suppliers grumbled in trade publications, anonymously of course, that the rollout was rushed and that few companies could justify the cost based on ROI. The technology was premature. Tags on products wrapped in foil or immersed in liquids were difficult, if not impossible, to read. Many tests showed no better than a 90-percent scan rate. But mostly it was the cost: a single RFID tag could run as high as fifty cents a pop. Not a big deal for high-margin products like televisions or pharmaceuticals, but a huge blow for peddlers of low-priced goods, where the margin on an entire pallet of, say, canned corn is obliterated by the cost of the tag. For large companies, the total bill for tags, printers, readers, technical expertise, and overall adjustments could be as high as $13–25 million.[23]

But since Wal-Mart was Wal-Mart, it was a diktat most suppliers could not turn away from and still stay in business. Noncompliance was not an option.[24]

When fully realized, RFID will make a global supply chain nearly transparent. Simply put, from the time it leaves the manufacturer until the point of sale in the store, Wal-Mart will be able to know with a reasonable degree of accuracy the whereabouts of its *entire* inventory. The 2005 rollout is just a baby step, mainly because it only requires tags to be placed on pallets. The ultimate goal is to have them on every product, something most RFID wonks see as a decade away, but the implications are staggering.

The initial gain for Wal-Mart will come in two places retailers systematically lose money: shrinkage (products stolen or lost on a supply chain) and "out-of-stocks." According to an Emory University study, items absent from the shelves cost retailers, on average, 4 percent of their annual sales.

"We know how many items are in the store, but we do not know where they are located," explains Linda Dillman. "Fully one-third of our inventory in a store is not on the shelf."[25] With RFID, a clerk could nail down missing items with ease, as readers can instantly determine where and when a product was last scanned.

In Wal-Mart's 1.1-million-square-foot distribution centers, finding mislabeled merchandise is like searching for a toothpick in a grain elevator. RFID creates a scenario in which a forklift operator will be instantly alerted should he attempt to place a pallet in the wrong stocking slot.

Hoping to allay concerns of suppliers spending millions on infrastructure with dubious expectation of returns, Wal-Mart is sure to note that it won't be the only one reaping the benefits. Cutting down on out-of-stocks and reducing shrinkage is mutually beneficial, they say. As is a visible supply chain. What's seldom mentioned is how it will cut labor costs and eliminate jobs. When readers can process multiple items, if not an entire shopping cart, in one fell swoop, cashiers will become obsolete. This can already be seen at many chain grocery stores where self-checkout kiosks offer more lanes without more personnel. Roughly half the aisles at Wal-Mart's emerging Neighborhood Markets are self-serve.

RFID's potential invokes the sort of imaginings once known only to science-fiction enthusiasts. For instance, some tags can gauge temperature, enabling the possibility of every milk carton having a custom sell-by date based on its temperature history from packaging plant to dairy case.

It took nearly a decade before an industry consensus could be established for barcodes. And it wasn't until the discounters took the plunge that the rest of retail followed suit. In thirty years, Wal-Mart has become an industry consensus unto itself. Where it goes, others follow, whether they want to or not.

SATELLITES TO PDAS

Inside a Wal-Mart, any Wal-Mart, a cashier is running low on five-dollar bills and receipt tape. Back in the old days of, uh, 2002, she'd have to flip on her red checkout light and hope its blinking would summon the attention of a nearby manager before her line came down with a case of register rage. Today, she only has to punch in a three-digit action code. The monitor then asks the following questions: "Bills or coins?" Then "1's-5's-10's-20's?" or "p-n-d-q?" for coinage. By answering the questions and hitting Enter, the cashier sends a message to a peripatetic customer-service manager (CSM, in Wal-Mart-ese), who receives it instantly on a PDA.

CSMs support the store's front-end operation. They back up the customer-service desk and make sure the cashiers stay up and running. Thanks to the action code, the CSM knows which cashier needs what kind of assistance. It's not always a question of fetching change. Should a glitch cause a cash drawer to lock up, no worries: a few taps on the PDA will pop it back open. Is nature making a call that can't be denied? The CSM can arrange cover for that, too.

Thanks to a technology first used by overscheduled CEOs, what once required three separate trips—one to assess the problem, another to round up the remedy (cash, roll tape, toilet plunger, etc.), and a third to bring the solution back to the register—has been combined into one. Cashiers can more quickly move customers out of the store while the CSMs are freed up to put out other fires.

This is Wal-Mart at its least controversial: using new technology to streamline its operation. For months or even years, it will hone and tweak and iron out the kinks before launching it chain wide. When you have over 5,000 stores worldwide, even the minutest cuts in time and effort have a ripple effect.

It's tempting to see retailing as somehow stagnant or stultifying. But the process by which products are shelved and merchandised, not to mention the thousands of chain reactions from tiny data connections, is as much a marvel as Ford's first assembly line. It's interesting that so much of the best of our creative energy benefits Wal-Mart first and last, and that it merely leads to the stocking of more "stuff."

The sheer shelving of so much disposable crap might trigger spasms of shame over our collective gluttony. What percentage of the contents of a 190,000-square-foot Supercenter will be in a landfill within a year? Does anyone really need a SpongeBob SquarePants popcorn tin? And the blinding brightness of fluorescent lights on Wal-Mart's white tile floors and the clinical blipping of hundreds and hundreds of sales, it's an environment ready-made for an extra-strength antidepressant. And that's just the stores. Witnessing Wal-Mart's social behavior might just lead you to the ledge.

FOUR

WAL-MARTS
BEHAVING BADLY, I

nlike Gap or Starbucks, Volkswagen or Apple, Wal-Mart does not sell brand lifestyle. Its architectural and advertising aesthetic is decidedly no-frills, its corporate offices stark. Executives pay for their own coffee. CEO Lee Scott shares hotel rooms on business trips. To curtail frivolous energy consumption, the lights, heat, and air conditioning at all 3,551 U.S. Wal-Marts are controlled from the Bentonville home office. Not surprisingly, this ethos of frugality hits those at the bottom of the food chain the hardest.

Essential to the Wal-Mart business model is keeping a choke collar on operating costs, one of the largest of which is, was, and always will be human labor. No matter how many times executives reveal their humility by getting down and wiggling to the Wal-Mart cheer, the stores depend on a constant stream of workers willing to work for wages that offer little prospect of becoming sustainable.

According to *Forbes,* the average Wal-Mart in-store employee makes roughly $7.50 an hour.* At that wage, an employee working full time would bring home around $18,000 a year, a number Wal-flack Mona Williams proudly confirmed to *Forbes* in 2004.[1] It's a wage, she says, that is "equal to what many union grocers pay and higher than at most other nonunion retailers."

Not quite. A scathing report from the U.S. House of Representatives' Committee on Education and the Workforce from 2004 has the average supermarket employee making $10.35 an hour. Compare that to the average wage Wal-Mart pays its employees.[2]

To put these figures in perspective, in 2003 Wal-Mart CEO Lee Scott made $4.3 million in salary and bonuses, and an additional $13.1 million in restricted stock grants.**[3]

PUNCHING THE CLOCK

Punching or "clocking" in to work remains part of the American lexicon, though that image is about as antiquated as the rotary telephone. These days Wal-Mart workers "swipe in" at the beginning of each shift with their magnetic-stripe ID badges. This ID card doesn't just identify; it tracks an associate's hours and wages using highly sophisticated software programs. This data is later printed out on

---

*Although some estimates claim the average wage is as high as $9.64 (which likely factors in those employees at the top of the food chain, like assistant managers), wages at Wal-Mart usually hover between $6.25 and $8.00 an hour.

**But perhaps Scott is the Wal-Mart employee of the retail giant executive world: that same year, Target's CEO made $23.1 million in salary, bonuses, and options, and Kmart's former president and chief executive officer Julian Day walked away from the company with an exit package worth over $100 million.

spreadsheets for final review. As high tech as the program is, how-ever, the information contained in it is easily altered.

Sometimes it's only a matter of shifting an hour from one week to the next in order to avoid overtime. In other cases it is far more insidious. One common practice is the "one-minute clock-out." This scam preys on the inevitability of human absentmindedness. Work-ers swipe out for lunch and then forget to clock back in. Instead of being paid for a six-hour shift, they receive pay for only half of it. The scam also preys on the vulnerabilities of those eking out a living on the lowest rungs of management, too scared to question the direct orders of a superior.[4]

Another example of how cost obsession subverts labor standards came to light in an audit leaked to the *New York Times*. Conducted by a Wal-Mart auditor in the summer of 2000, and kept under court seal for almost four years, the audit detailed thousands of cases in which minors worked during school hours and longer than legally allowed. It also reported more than 60,000 instances of employees' failing to take breaks. The audit investigated only 128 different Wal-Marts and Sam's Clubs, which in 2000 represented just 4 percent of the com-pany's fleet. Despite the prolificacy of lawsuits alleging different ver-sions of essentially the same story, Wal-Mart dismissed its audit as meaningless. Describing the methodology as "flawed," Mona Williams claimed the numbers evidenced only instances of its workers' being forgetful and not recording their breaks.[5]

Former employees tell a different story. One former manager, Joyce Moody, told the *New York Times* that the company had "threatened to write up managers if they didn't bring the payroll low enough." Managers were instructed to keep their labor costs at 8 percent of sales at the most; they then leaned on their own assistant managers to force employees to work off the clock or, unbelievably, to simply delete hours from employees' timesheets.[6] In February of

2004, a federal jury in Oregon found that Wal-Mart had forced eighty-three employees to work unpaid overtime between 1994 and 1999.

Wal-Mart combines cost savings with employee intimidation through the unusual practice of overnight lock-ins. According to the *New York Times,* which broke the story in January 2004, approximately 10 percent of Wal-Marts and Sam's Clubs lock the door on their overnight crews. Although it's hardly a common practice among retailers, Wal-Mart claims it's done to protect employees working in high-crime areas. Individual store managers who're under no obligation to bolster their decision with crime stats determine whether or not a crew is locked in.

Locking the overnight shift in not only deters shrinkage but also keeps employees from sneaking outside for breaks, or "time theft" as Wal-Mart calls it. In several instances Wal-Mart associates became violently ill or suffered an accident on the job. So grave was the threat of termination for any worker opening a fire door absent a real fire that many writhed in pain for hours rather than open the door themselves.[7]

Among the workers most affected by this kind of labor practice are illegal immigrants. In the fall of 2003, a grand jury was convened to consider bringing labor racketeering charges against Wal-Mart executives for knowingly hiring illegal immigrants. Although Wal-Mart blamed the agencies that it contracted with for the presence of illegals in its workforce, federal investigators had executives on tape— in wiretapped conversations—confirming they knew the workers were illegal.[8]

EVERYDAY NO HEALTH CARE

While other companies have long acquiesced to the consensus that health insurance is an entitlement of employment, perhaps even a moral imperative, Wal-Mart sees it as one more checkout item. As Lee Scott "carefully" explained to CNBC, "Part of the reason that we have health-care costs like we do is because it's one of the few areas in our life where we are not good consumers. We're not shopping for reasonableness or anything else because we're not paying any of the money. And Sam [Walton] believed that we should, as individuals, pay some of that cost, so that we would be able to be enlisted to support the efforts to control the costs of health care."[9]

At Wal-Mart, health insurance is available only after six months' uninterrupted employment for full-timers and after two years for part-timers, who may not insure spouses or children. Wal-Mart then changed the definition of part-time from twenty-eight to thirty-four hours a week at a time when approximately a full third of its workforce was part-time.[10] The report of the House of Representatives' Committee on Education and the Workforce found that "a single worker could end up spending around $6,400 out-of-pocket—about 45 percent of her annual full-time salary—before seeing a single benefit from the health plan."[11]

Associates insuring a spouse eligible for coverage must pay a "spouse surcharge" of $50 per two-week pay period, in addition to the monthly fees for spousal coverage.

Also consider what Wal-Mart will *not* pay for:

- contraceptives
- childhood vaccinations
- dental checkups

- flu shots
- and many preexisting conditions during the first year of employment[12]

Topping it off is that even after all the premiums and deductibles, workers still pay 20 percent of medical costs up to $1,750, a grand total of 42 percent of their healthcare costs.[13] This number borders on unconscionable when you take into consideration that, nationally, employees of large companies like Wal-Mart pay, on average, 16 percent of their premiums.

For workers hoping to get the most from their hard-earned insurance, catastrophic illness is the way to go. Unlike almost half of employer-funded plans in the country, Wal-Mart pays 100 percent of costs above $1,750, with no lifetime caps. This has resulted in Bentonville's shelling out big-time million-dollar-plus organ transplants.[14] A major fringe benefit of this emergency-only approach is that it comes with built-in bragging rights. This much was made explicit in a particularly nauseating episode of its "Good Jobs" TV propaganda campaign in which a young couple describe the plight of their disease-ridden infant son who by the grace of Wal-Mart breathes today.

What goes unsaid is that, as *Los Angeles Times* journalist Michael Hiltzik discovered, these sorts of transplants are needed by around one hundredth of one percent (0.01 percent) of the company's insured employees. Hiltzik writes: "By steering coverage towards major procedures over routine benefits, which would be used by a huge percentage of employees, Wal-Mart has turned a couple of decades of health-care orthodoxy on its head."[15]

So what does all this mean for Wal-Mart's bottom line? Like everything else, it means more money. What does it mean for the country? For one, as standard-bearer for corporate America, Wal-

Mart has set a dangerously low standard of employee treatment that might possibly impel other companies of its ilk to take the same approach in order to compete. This is exactly what happened in California in 2004, when 59,000 unionized grocery employees went on strike to protest higher healthcare costs demanded of them by their employers. The reason that healthcare costs had to go up, the grocery chains insisted, was that this was their only means of keeping pace with Wal-Mart.

Another troubling result of this sort of labor practice is that it costs us money. By making health coverage for low-wage employees exorbitantly expensive, Wal-Mart pretty much insures that most of its associates will look elsewhere for medical care or simply do without. Where they often end up, however, is the public doorstep. Wal-Mart's so-called "quality health insurance" often translates into a public handout. An increasing number of states are finding out the hard way that inviting Wal-Mart may mean more jobs, but it also means more names on the welfare rolls. For example:

- In Georgia, nearly 10,000 children of Wal-Mart–employed parents were enrolled in PeachCare, Georgia's public health-insurance program—more than from any other company in the state by a factor of ten. Estimated cost of Wal-Mart to state and federal taxpayers in 2002: $6.6 million.[16]

- In 2004, a North Carolina hospital claimed that of 1,900 patients who were also Wal-Mart employees, 31 percent of them were on Medicaid. Another 16 percent had no insurance.[17]

- In Wisconsin, Wal-Mart employees and their dependents rack up an annual bill of $4.75 million, through a combination of their use of the state's "BadgerCare" insurance for low-income working families and Medicaid. According to numbers from the state's health department, 3,765 Wal-Mart associates and their dependents receive public assistance.[18]

- In Tennessee, 25 percent of Wal-Mart's 37,000 employees were enrolled in TennCare, the state's public health system. Wal-Mart topped the state's roster of private corporations with most employees on the public dole. In its mode of reflexive denial, Wal-Mart claimed its health plan was not designed to be bolstered by the state. "It's just the law of large numbers," a Wal-flack explained to the *Knoxville News-Sentinel*.[19]

- In California, documents released as part of the *Dukes vs. Wal-Mart* gender-discrimination suit revealed that researchers found that the average non-salaried Wal-Mart associate takes in nearly $2,000 in public welfare benefits each year (including health care, food stamps, and subsidized housing). If all of California's retailers lowered their wages to Wal-Mart's level, the cost to the state could reach over $400 million.

- California taxpayers bore the burden of an estimated $20.5 million worth of medical care—effectively a subsidy for Wal-Mart—for the company's employees in 2003.[20] Unbelievably, according to Sylvia Chase of *NOW with Bill Moyers*, Wal-Mart personnel managers *encourage* workers to apply for public assistance.[21]

California decided to do something about it. Or it tried to. Proposition 72 was one of more than a dozen ballot measures on the sprawling 2004 California ballot. It was less a new proposal than an electoral ratification of a bill passed under former governor Gray

Davis. If passed, however, it had the potential to radically improve the lives of millions of uninsured Californians. The brainchild of state senator John Burton (D), Prop 72 required businesses with more than 200 employees to cover 80 percent of workers' healthcare costs.

Not surprisingly, the California Chamber of Commerce, numerous school districts, many newspapers, and a host of midsized businesses actively fought the measure. The most prominent opponent of the measure, however, was (no surprise) Wal-Mart. The company dumped half a million dollars into the fight in the hopes the measure would go down in flames.

"Many of our opponents are trying to use the political system to stop our growth," Bob McAdam, Wal-Mart's vice president of corporate affairs told the Associated Press. "And we are not going to sit back and take it without responding. We will respond."[22]

Opponents of Prop 72 wisely framed the measure not as a means of saving Wal-Mart, which, at the time, employed about 60,000 Californians. Rather, it was a fight for "small businesses" and "consumers" interested in healthcare choices against the restrictive power of big government. Thanks to a ballot measure supporting stem cell research—one that triggered vociferous opposition from the reactionary churches of George W. Bush and Mel Gibson alike—Prop 72 did not enjoy a terrific amount of national attention. However, in California, the airwaves were full of anti–Prop 72 screeds, as well as a few pro–Prop 72 commercials.

Perhaps the most audacious comment from Wal-Mart regarding its health-benefits package came from Susan Chambers, the executive vice president who oversees benefits at Wal-Mart. On the eve of the vote, in response to charges of, in the words of the *New York Times,* its "miserly approach to employee health care," Chambers dismissed the criticism by saying "You can't solve it for the 1.2 million associates if you can't solve it for the country."[23]

Hmmm . . . 360 million people versus a workforce of 1.2 million, and Wal-Mart is throwing its hands up? Where are its famously intense initiative and creative problem-solving skills? Maybe they're MIA because this is not a problem Wal-Mart wants to solve.

Proposition 72 was soundly defeated. In the wake of the ballot defeat, Wal-flack Cynthia Lin declared that "Prop 72 was never about Wal-Mart. It was about allowing businesses to operate without unreasonable government mandates, it was about the survival of small businesses, and it was about consumer choice in health care benefits."[24] Irony is seldom so perfect.

WELFARE SMILEY

American workers at the turn of the millennium have been treated to a triple dose of bad luck and bitchslap: economic recession, a remarkably jobless recovery, and skyrocketing health-insurance costs. Between 2000 and 2004, employee health-insurance costs shot up by 36 percent. The number of Americans spending a quarter or more of their incomes on health care rose from 11.6 to 14.3 million in 2004.[25] Even in large corporations, the percentage of workers with company-offered insurance declined from 71 to 66 percent.[26] But most disturbing, the population of the uninsured swelled to a record *45 million*.

Across the country, activists have been successful in pushing "living wage" ordinances in approximately 110 cities and counties since the mid-1990s.[27] This push (*The Nation* in 2003 optimistically called it a "countermovement"[28]) would require companies wanting into a community to provide employees a living wage, one that often exceeds the minimum wage by a few dollars. In exchange, the companies would get the public subsidy medley from the city that they now expect even without the promise of good wages. This tack requires, of course, due vigilance on the part of the average citizen; city officials often salivate over new development and economic interest. Such was the case with St. Paul, capital of the normally good-sensed state of Minnesota. In 2001, the city council waived its living-wage policy—one the council itself created—in order to lure Target into its downtown. (Along with the free pass on living wages, St. Paul handed Target a $6.3 million subsidy.[29])

In Chicago, New York, and Los Angeles, politicians and activists have thrown the ball of social responsibility back into Bentonville's court. To do business here, they say, you'll have to step up and pay workers responsibly. For the most part, Wal-Mart has balked at this.

Depending on your politics, such gestures are either organized extortion, brilliant political organizing, or the complex machinations of democracy itself. One thing's painfully clear: Rather than concede to a living wage, or stay neutral should its associates choose to associate into a union, Wal-Mart has put its tail between its legs and begged off like a bitch.

FIVE

WAL-MARTS
BEHAVING BADLY, II

G ot any nachos ready?" That's what Joe Hendrix said to the folks at the Radio Grill, his employer's in-house snack bar. Hendrix was on his way to punch out from his shift in the meat-cutting department at the Wal-Mart Supercenter in Jacksonville, Texas. Eight months earlier, in February 2000, he'd voted yes in the first election for union representation at a U.S. Wal-Mart store. For failing to pay when placing his nacho order, he was fired.

Seventy-two-year-old Sidney Smith also voted yes; he got axed for eating a preweighed banana on the checkout line. Such were the excuses offered by management as union supporters were systematically routed from their jobs. But this was well after the real damage had been done, when Wal-Mart announced two weeks after the

Jacksonville vote that it was switching to case-ready, or precut, beef and would be eliminating meat-cutting operations in 180 stores.

A similar narrative unfolded in the fall of 2004 at a Wal-Mart in Jonquière, Canada, when a majority of workers signed cards authorizing representation by the United Food and Commercial Workers (UFCW). An hour and a half north of Quebec City, the region has long been a union power base, with pulp mills laying the foundation for successive generations of union members. Because of the province's unique labor laws, the union was able to gain authorization by collecting signed cards from a majority of the workforce instead of having to go through a formal election, which provides management with time to endlessly dispute the makeup of the unit. (For instance, Wal-Mart often insists that its managers are no different from hourly workers and therefore should be allowed to vote.)

It seemed a straightforward organizing campaign, a successful one, and the government certified the Jonquière union and set a timetable for the two sides to start negotiating.

Then Wal-Mart announced that the Jonquière store was losing money and would likely have to close, citing the "fractured environment" created by the union campaign. With workers at two other Wal-Marts elsewhere in the province preparing a similar organizing drive, along with several more in British Columbia, the sudden closing of a store that had not, to anyone's knowledge, previously been in trouble financially was a strong message to those hoping to unionize.

"Fear is really the issue, and who wins on that issue wins the campaign," says Mike Leonard, a retired UFCW vice president. "I don't know that there's more fear in retail. I think that it's deeper and that there may be more of it at Wal-Mart, because people absolutely know what they're up against."[1]

In the case of the Jacksonville meat-cutters, Wal-Mart claimed its decision had nothing to do with the organizing drive, but the union filed a complaint with the National Labor Relations Board. Although the board ruled in the union's favor, the timing of the news (about the shutdown of meat-cutting operations) served as a chillingly clear message to Wal-Mart workers nationwide: This is what you can expect if you try to organize. Reinforcing this point five years later, Wal-Mart shuttered its store in Jonquière, Quebec, just four months after workers voted to join the UFCW. Wal-Mart claimed the UFCW's demands would render the store unprofitable, while the union claimed the move was pure power politics designed to frighten workers already organizing at Wal-Marts throughout Canada.

Wal-Mart's legendary ferocity in such situations has, until relatively recently, kept unions from trying to make inroads in its million-strong workforce. But after more than a decade of pussyfooting, the UFCW has been gearing up to take on Wal-Mart.

For the UFCW, this undertaking is less the result of newfound militancy than it is about mere survival. Seventy percent of the union's 1.4 million members work for national groceries like Kroger and Safeway, as well as for smaller regional chains. With a strong presence in the top one hundred mostly urban markets, the big chains can hold steady in the face of Wal-Mart encroachment. The regional chains, however, are getting walloped. And with Wal-Mart circling on the fringes of larger markets, its lower wages and benefits will likely erode those enjoyed by UFCW members.

The only Wal-Mart store to unionize successfully was in Ontario, Canada, abetted in no small measure by the province's once progressive labor laws. But the fledgling union was broken by the company's flat-out refusal to recognize the contract. While a climber at a Mount Everest base camp can turn his thoughts to the many individuals who have summited and lived, a Wal-Mart worker trying to join a union enjoys no such consolation. The UFCW, hardly a paragon of union democracy or member mobilization, faces an employer that has been growing by 15 percent each year, recession and all. In the context of a labor movement that has not been weaker since the 1920s, and with a legal system seemingly rigged against it, this is an Everest ascent with no Sherpas in sight.

UNIONFREE AND LOVIN' IT

Sam Walton has been dead for a decade, but he lives on as the customer-service superego of Wal-Martians nationwide. The myth of "Mr. Sam" as a benign patriarch is so pervasive that rather than contradict it, the UFCW plays along, with campaign messages about "restoring Sam's vision."

But Walton's vision never included unions.

As *Wall Street Journal* reporter Bob Ortega chronicles in his book *In Sam We Trust,* Walton was bent on maintaining low labor costs and paying workers subminimum wages when he could get away with it, and he showed no qualms about threatening store and warehouse closures to beat back union campaigns. The company's trumpeted profit-sharing plan and "open door policy" for addressing grievances were all born out of the pleading of Walton's union-busting con-sigliere, John Tate. Tate believed that Walton could circumvent labor problems by convincing his workers that he was on their side. For Walton, this turned out to be a winning strategy: a full-time union-prevention program.

A perpetually churning workforce offers the added benefit, from management's perspective, of keeping the union out. By its own admission, Wal-Mart burns through more than half of all new hires each year—a lot of people in a workforce of over a million. As Bernie Hesse of UFCW Local 789 in the Twin Cities explains, the paradox of retail organizing is: "I'm working retail. This job sucks. If I don't like it, I'll go get another job that pays $6.50 an hour." While many retail workers don't see their jobs as being worth a long, arduous battle for representation, they also shrink from the consequences of support- ing a union: demotions, reductions in hours, and "Got any nachos ready?" firings.

Since the UFCW began talking to meat-cutters en masse in 1999, Wal-Mart's People Division (the branch responsible for Human Re- sources strategy and programs for its workforce) has increased from twelve employees to nearly seventy. In terms of preparedness, though, Wal- Mart has always trumped the unions. Before any national campaign was afoot, Wal-Mart was already publishing and distributing manuals like "A Manager's Toolbox to Remaining Union Free," producing videos and running two-day workshops for store managers, stressing their role as the "first line of defense" against a union campaign.

On paper Wal-Mart stays within the bounds of how an employer can legally respond to a union drive. "They're cosmetics," says union- buster turned union adviser Martin Levitt. "The company will wave them like a flag to show that they know the law, but once manage- ment and supervisors have been pulled into one-on-one meetings with the union-busting forces, they are carefully programmed on how to break the law and told clearly that their very job depends on doing so."

While a store manager may have been briefed on extralegal maneuvers, the dirty work is often delegated to nonsalaried depart- ment managers with no knowledge of labor law. Gretchen Adams, a comanager at a Las Vegas Supercenter, was instructed by her district manager not to hire anyone with union experience, while Stan Fortune, a former department manager and security guard, was told to solicit grievances from union supporters, implementing raises and promotions to buy their loyalty. "I never knew I was breaking the law," he says. Former Wal-Mart spokeswoman Jessica Moser Eldred said the company follows all state, federal, and local labor laws. "In no circumstance do we deviate from them."

Part of Wal-Mart's strategy is to deny contact between workers and the union. When it owns the land on which its store sits, it will invoke trespassing laws. "It got to the point where as soon as the organizers got out of their cars, the security guards would be in the parking lots telling them to leave," says former cashier Alan Peto.

In other cases, managers or security guards shadow organizers throughout the store, making it impossible for them to speak to workers. Organizers from the UFCW international staff are currently barred from all Wal-Marts under an injunction that forbids solicitation. The company has infuriated shoppers suspected of being union organizers by ejecting them; they've even booted Girl Scouts and Salvation Army bell ringers for fear that bending its no-solicitation policy will give the union an inroad. Faced with the inevitable litany of unfair-labor-practice charges from the union in response to its maneuverings, Wal-Mart can count on the glacial pace of the labor board to stall the campaign. If the board rules in the union's favor, the company suffers a slap on the wrist, posting a notice of company malfeasance in the break room. This is union organizing still haunted by the ghost of the Taft-Hartley Act.

ORGANIZE WAL-MART!
UH, OKAY . . . HOW?

Just for shits and giggles, dial (479) 273-8300. That's Wal-Mart's twenty-four-hour "Union Hotline," designed for store managers to call on the first whiff of union activity. Your kind message will activate the beeper of an associate in Wal-Mart's People Division. Assuming you are a store manager (and not a pinko prankster), your call will be promptly returned. If your associates are talking union, a flying column of union-busters will be instantly dispatched to put out the fire.

Bentonville's hit squad engages in the tried-and-true tactics of sowing division through fear and intimidation. Managers follow workers closely, often isolating them individually to gauge their level of support—or even the potential for a yes vote. A "Vote No" committee emerges in a way that makes it seem like a grassroots, wholly organic activity. Wal-Mart won't pay a livable wage, but it sure as hell finds money for VOTE NO stickers and buttons. Workers are also forced to watch antiunion videos and listen to speeches from the Bentonville staff. (Wal-Mart claims these videos are meant to "educate their associates about labor law.")

Union-buster talking points have changed little over the past three decades. They usually go something like this: Unions are needless third parties antithetical to the corporate culture; they're interested only in collecting dues from workers and forcing strikes; contract negotiations put "everything" on the table, and "you may get more or you may get less"; the union can't guarantee you a thing. Wal-Mart also expertly frames the issues in such a way that workers who vote against unionization are cast as independent thinkers who handle problems on their own. "I can speak for myself," is Wal-Mart's slogan of choice.[2]

Finally, the decline in union membership on the national level is often presented as proof positive that unions are a thing of the past. And, sadly, the company may have a point: in the 1950s, 35 percent of American workers belonged to unions. Now only 12 percent claim membership. In the private sector the percentage has dipped below 9 percent. And yet in countless surveys, nearly 50 percent of workers say they would join a union if the option were available.

The doublespeak propaganda Wal-Mart showers on workers and the press might as well equate unions with hula hoops—a thing of the past. It wasn't the devastating decline of unionized industries like steel and manufacturing that was the problem. Workers simply came to their senses, pulled a Norma Rae in reverse, and ripped up their union cards.[3]

The challenge to unionize Wal-Mart comes at a time of unprecedented weakness for the labor movement. For all the millions in campaign contributions labor pours into Democratic coffers, unions get thank-you notes in the form of NAFTA. In only one of the eight years of Clinton rule, did labor see its decline come to a temporary halt. The other "greatest generation" that stuck its collective neck out for labor in the thirties and forties is finding its way to the great Walter Reuther Retirement Home in the sky. And in a country that treats its history like a massive Etch A Sketch, today's workers have come to see hard-won gains as entitlements.

A steady erosion in wages and benefits has fostered a climate of despair. Nowhere is this more true than in retail. Even among unionized workers, an employer triumph is often considered inevitable.

WORKERS OR REAL ESTATE?

America's historic labor victories occurred in industries like steel, auto-making, trucking, and mining, and they were often bloody, protracted fights. But the advantage unions held over the big employers was a centralized workforce. A single factory might employ hundreds, even thousands of workers. A victory in one plant had huge implications for all the others.

Setting aside the symbolic value of the few Wal-Marts that have successfully unionized in Canada,* to succeed at organizing one of

---

*Wal-Mart entered Canada in 1994 by acquiring 122 Woolco discount stores. Notably absent from the deal were the chain's ten unionized stores.

Wal-Mart's 3,551 U.S. stores is essentially meaningless. In Canada, workers claim Wal-Mart has refused to honor labor contracts or has simply dragged the process out in the courts and the labor board until the prounion workers quit in frustration. And of course Wal-Mart can simply close a problematic store with minimal effect to its sales.

The question of how, or even if, Wal-Mart can be organized has long been a contentious one in labor circles. As early as the mid-eighties, the union was aware that Wal-Mart was a juggernaut they couldn't long afford to ignore. Jeff Fiedler of the AFL-CIO's Food and Allied Service Trades division was among the first to sound the alarm by talking to dozens of UFCW locals.

"Generally we were criticized for being too late, but we were early," Fiedler explains. "One of the problems was that Wal-Mart was putting its stores near nonunion competitors; their early significant growth was largely in nonunion areas. They were not a presence in union markets." This, according to Fiedler, led to a false sense of security among many UFCW leaders. "It was human nature. People didn't believe us. At the time, it was 'They're not into food, it's not a problem.'"

From the late eighties through most of the nineties, the UFCW fought Wal-Mart by publicizing its malfeasance and by supporting communities trying to hold it at bay. In the former they were extremely successful. Jeff Fiedler was largely responsible for much of the research into Wal-Mart's factories in Bangladesh, which he promptly fed to producers at *Dateline NBC,* who would go on to humiliate CEO David Glass in 1992. The union also started a short-lived campaign to pressure the company into buying more domestically made shoes.

Absent from the UFCW efforts, however, was any actual organizing. At the time, UFCW officials acknowledged a campaign as premature, even though Wal-Mart's Supercenters were starting to take market share. As Mike Leonard sees it, this proved to be a mistake.

"The idea was, at the leadership level, 'We'll just keep them from building their stores.' Protect market share, protect market share. We still have people who think that was a good idea. But Safeway or Albertsons has never given the workers a raise and said 'Hey, you did a good job keeping them out.' The mission of the union is to go out and fight for the workers, all these issues [i.e., sprawl, protecting small businesses] are valid, [but] I think that other people do that better than us."[4]

Disconnect between members of the UFCW and its leadership arguably played a role in the disaster of the California grocery strike. At the sad end of the four-month struggle, despite a contract that offered cuts in wages and benefits, UFCW International president Doug Dority inexplicably hailed it as "one of the most successful strikes in U.S. history." This defender of the proletariat earned more than $300,000 in salary and another $50,000 in disbursement in 2003. A day after declaring victory, he retired to split time between his two homes, in Florida and Colorado. Like Scott and his cashier associates, having workers' best interests at heart might not be a foregone conclusion.*

Another UFCW higher-up, Jack Loveall, presides over Local 588 in Roseville, California, which represents 17,000 workers. In 2002, Loveall gave himself a $100,000 raise, so that he was making nearly a half million dollars a year. His staff includes five family members and two pilots to fly them around in the union's private jet. The union also pays for his country club membership so that he can "talk business."

---

*This has not gone unnoticed among UFCW members, and in the Internet's anonymous wilderness, they have been bitching. The ability for workers to talk to each other is terrifying to union leaders: the dirty secrets can't be hidden, the ridiculous salaries are exposed, and workers can educate themselves using message boards and websites.

According to LM-2 statements filed by the UFCW in 2003, the union has twenty-four vice presidents with salaries over $200,000 a year. Of the thirty union officers in the entire nation who earn more than $300,000, seven hail from the UFCW.*[5]

Some labor leaders like Service Employees International Union president Andy Stern have begun suggesting, however indirectly, that perhaps the UFCW isn't up for the job of taking on Wal-Mart. Shortly after the 2004 elections Stern call for the AFL-CIO to radically consolidate from its sixty-plus member unions to ten or twelve überunions. He also proposed devoting an entire AFL-CIO division to organizing Wal-Mart. Whether this is a power play or a path to power remains to be seen. It's certainly stirred things up with politicians and union wonks, but does reshuffling the bureaucracy really do anything? Does a single Wal-Mart associate really care? Pinch-hitting another union for the increasingly inept UFCW, however, certainly can't hurt the chances of an organized Wal-Mart within a generation.

And yet some caution that the movement is simply too weak to justify an expensive campaign that offers little hope of victory in the foreseeable future: Is it a good gamble for workers who risk losing their jobs if they show support for the union, let alone vote yes in an election? But, increasingly, more in the labor movement are beginning to see that Wal-Mart's business practices and its labor policies are bleeding into other industries. Labor doesn't have the luxury of waiting for the historical moment to ripen. Wal-Mart must be attacked, whether the movement is ready or not.

*The list of thirty union officers also includes presidents of unions such as the Major League Baseball Players Association, the Federation of Professional Athletes, and the Air Line Pilots Association, all with memberships whose earnings trump the average grocery clerk's by many a mile.

REAPING WHAT YOU SOW

In the sixteen years since Wal-Mart opened its first Supercenter, the UFCW has run a damage-control campaign bent on stemming the tide of expansion and sullying the company's image. The union has helped call attention to Wal-Mart's use of sweatshops and child labor overseas, as well as its bogus "Buy American" program, where the company wrapped itself in a "Made in the U.S.A." flag until it was revealed that most of its apparel was made in overseas sweatshops. The union also forged coalitions with antisprawl activists to stem Wal-Mart's growth.

All of these are noble pursuits, but without a strategy to organize workers they're about as effective as pummeling the Taliban with passages from *The Betty Friedan Reader.* Until recently it was hard to tell if the UFCW was boycotting Wal-Mart, organizing it, or simply functioning as a thorn in its side. This mixed message provided the People Division an opportunity to inoculate its associates with videos like *Wal-Mart Under Attack,* which shows footage of UFCW rallies with members chanting "Wal-Mart—not in my neighborhood" and highlights various local efforts to get union members to sign pledges not to shop at Wal-Mart. The message that the union is against Wal-Mart is an effective means of turning workers against it from the get-go.

VIVA LAS VEGAS?

In the spring of 2004, after more than two years of attempting to organize Wal-Marts and Sam's Clubs in the union-friendly city of Las Vegas, the UFCW threw in the towel. The union dissolved its

Department of Strategic Programs, which conducted most of the campaign's research and outreach, and the half-dozen former Wal-Mart managers who had been recruited as organizers were dismissed.[6]

It was a devastating blow to those who had hoped for unionization, and who had worked hard to make it happen. But it had been, admittedly, a tough road. In November 2001, workers at Las Vegas Sam's Club Store 6382 were set to vote in what was the third storewide election at a U.S. Wal-Mart. But as the election approached, the company went into a hiring frenzy, disrupting the laboratory conditions required by the National Labor Relations Board. Watching its support ebb as the company packed the unit with new hires—all of whom were subjected to antiunion videos and meetings—the union filed charges, which resulted in the board's decision to block the election. On March 28, 2002, the NLRB issued a complaint against the company, but the best the union is likely to get is a rescheduled election with little to guarantee that Wal-Mart won't do the same thing again.

The UFCW, for its part, has taken a largely top-down approach to the campaign, which has been guided by pressure tactics coming from union HQ in Washington—with some exceptions. "I get members asking me how it's going, how many people have signed cards, and I say what's the point? Why go through a regular election just to get knocked down?" says UFCW organizer Bernie Hesse. "I'm not trying to go store by store; I'm trying to build a social movement." Hesse's Local 789 has launched a campaign for retail workers in the Twin Cities called "You Are Worth More." Rather than hone in on one particular company, Hesse's local is planting roots in the community, establishing itself as a presence among a multiracial workforce at metro-area Targets, Kmarts, and Wal-Marts.

Its great fun to imagine a blue-vest revolt: the airwaves of Wal-

Mart TV hijacked by prounion messages; the store PA system telling customers to leave immediately, the doors locking behind them; every hour that the Supercenter is closed, Wal-Mart loses sales—thousands—and Bentonville's teradata system could tally the cost of lost shopping hours down to the last cent.

It's a fantasy for sure, lefty porn that makes Michael Moore look vanilla. But somewhere between new dreams and new ideas a brighter day for Wal-Mart workers will be born. Whether there's an AFL-CIO around to welcome the million-plus members into the fold is anyone's guess.

Wal-Mart is likely to be a decades-long struggle, one fought by a workforce with no union experience. As of now, however, the war is being waged by a vanguard of union lawyers. Ultimately the suits will have to take a backseat to shop-floor workers, member organizers, and, most significant, the communities where workers live. When the distinctions between union and community collapse, the employer's traditional mode of attack—labeling the union an alien third party—disintegrates and the campaign becomes less dependent on legal wrangling. Then, when Wal-Mart denies workers access to the union, wrecks an election, or fires activist workers, the outraged response comes not from a lone UFCW mouthpiece but from an entire movement.

Given this campaign's stakes—both real and symbolic—a movement is what Wal-Mart workers need.

"If these retailers are going to be the jobs of the future, if we've really switched from a production to a service economy, than what is so revolutionary about insisting that they pay a living wage?" Hesse asks. Millions of associates and citizens may have to ask this question a million more times before a movement becomes something tangible, and not just a feel-good progressive mirage.

THE WAL-MART EFFECT

The biggest strike in California's history was a parade of hopes, horrors, and massive confusion. Seventy thousand workers from the Tijuana border north to San Luis Obispo faced down the combined muscle of three of the largest grocery corporations in the country: Safeway, Albertsons, and Kroger. But workers were also staring down another beast, one notably absent from the negotiations.

In 2002, with Wal-Mart's announced plans to open forty Supercenters in California over the next three years, the former big guns of the grocery biz started sweating. How could they compete, they wondered. The answer for Safeway, Albertsons, and Kroger was to slash benefits. And so without even a single petition drive or media charm offensive, Wal-Mart helped facilitate one of organized labor's saddest defeats in recent memory.

Taking an ass-whupping from Wal-Mart across the country, the "big three" of Safeway, Albertsons, and Kroger decided they had to demand concessions from their workers or become another Wal-Mart casualty. Negotiations stalled and started and stalled again. Finally, in October 2003, the big three's contract, which offered workers no wage increases and a substantial hike in their health insurance payments, was overwhelmingly rejected.

A union grocery worker can do well in southern California, where wages average around $14 an hour. It's not get-rich money, but it's nothing to scoff at, especially at a time when fully paid health care is being redefined as decadence. Most California grocery workers are part-timers for whom health insurance is easily the biggest perk of employment. Prior to October 2003, the big three paid the whole tab for their employees' health insurance. But citing rising insurance costs and competitive pressure from Wal-Mart, they held firm to their new position. The fifty-year reign of employer-paid coverage was at its end. Concede or suffer the consequences.

The strike kicked off with an employee walkout at Vons, a subsidiary of Safeway. Safeway and Ralphs (owned by Kroger) retaliated by locking workers out, and the battle lines were quickly drawn. The strike enjoyed popular support from customers, other unions, and the public at large. What the unions didn't know then was that the California attorney general's office would later investigate the big three for an alleged illegal profit-sharing scheme to help weather the massive loss of business due to the strike. Ironically, some pickets actually diverted business to nearby Wal-Marts.

Cooperation with both the Teamsters and the AFL-CIO was just as mottled. When pickets went up at grocery distribution centers, Teamster trucks crossed the line. A month later, they started honoring the pickets until, for reasons never thoroughly explained, they received the go-ahead to cross them again a month later. The UFCW called in the AFL-CIO to strategize, but then pushed them back out later. The workers courageously held the line, but after twenty weeks, the prospect of personal debt and no health insurance at all was just too much. What they settled for in February 2004 was little better than the original offer they had rejected twenty weeks earlier. As one worker summed it up in the *New York Times,* "I don't worry about me," she said. "But with treatment like this from the company, with this kind of contract, the middle class is just becoming the lower class. But I'll vote for it. I want to go back to work."[7]

It's a chilling defeat for unionized workers of smaller chain stores who are trying to stay out of the way of the impending Wal-Mart tsunami. The pressure faced by stores like Kroger and Safeway will translate—and already has—into diminished benefits and lower wages, and other employment policies that the union would once have laughed at but that are becoming the best offer they can get.

OUR PATRIARCHY
MAKES THE DIFFERENCE

In recent years Wal-Mart's image has been inextricably caught up in its "women problems." On June 22, 2004, a federal judge certified the largest class-action lawsuit in American history, *Dukes vs. Wal-Mart*. The suit covers every woman hired by the company since 1998, an estimated 1.6 million associates. One federal judge likened the case to 1954's *Brown vs. Board of Education*. The suit alleges unequal wage and promotion policies for women. Women at Wal-Mart were paid an average of 6.2 percent less than male employees. In addition, a full two-thirds of Wal-Mart's hourly employees are female; but women fill only one-third of all managerial positions.[8]

The thousands of depositions taken from Wal-Mart women reflect a variety of experiences with and attitudes toward the company. Several of the lead plaintiffs are still employed by Wal-Mart and stress that they believe in the company's alleged mission of "raising the standard of living." Central to their testimony is how Wal-Mart fostered a climate in which women trying to ascend the ranks of management were subtly discouraged and flat-out refused by a boy's club of store managers and district managers whose attitudes toward the fairer sex could safely be categorized as mullah-lite.

Some of the more egregious instances involve an eighteen-year associate being told she'd have to "doll up" in order to get promoted.

"The more I complained," she said, "the more they considered me the big bad B-word."[9]

Another assistant manager happened upon a male colleague's W-2 form, which revealed that he was paid $10,000 more for doing the same job. When she brought it up with her store manager, she was told he had a family to support, even though she was a single mother. When she wanted a raise, her manager asked that she submit a household budget to justify such an increase.

One plaintiff in the suit, a single mother with four children, was hired at Wal-Mart in 1990, making $3.85 an hour. She begged for further training and requested promotions, but eight years later, she was only making $7.32 an hour; it took her seven years to reach management level. All around her, her male counterparts were awarded promotions and raises.[10]

That Wal-Mart had women trouble was common knowledge long before *Dukes*. Sam Walton admitted as much in his memoir, noting how moving up management ranks required sudden and frequent relocation, something he confessed was usually more of an obstacle for women. His wife, Helen, who he confessed was "a bit of a feminist," and daughter Alice, a successful investor, helped hip old man Walton to the problem. At their insistence, he appointed a woman to Wal-Mart's board of directors in 1986. As that woman would later recall, the tap from Mr. Sam went something like this: "I think I need a woman; would you like to be her?" The woman in question was none other than Hillary Clinton, an attorney with the Rose Law Firm in Little Rock.[11] It just so happened that her husband was the governor of Arkansas.

OUR SWEATSHOPS MAKE THE DIFFERENCE

American retailers have long been a reluctant bunch when it comes to crossing national borders. The cost of real estate, restrictive trade rules, and cultural differences in tastes and manners all force a potentially painful rethink of a proven formula. Wal-Mart, however, has been aggressively crossing borders for more than a decade. Since

establishing its first Mexican outpost in 1991, it has opened for business in nine countries on four continents. In the United Kingdom,
its acquisition of the ASDA chain has made it the second-largest
retailer in that country, while ASDA's George line of apparel has put
it at the number-one slot in clothing. In Brazil, Wal-Mart has
climbed to the number-three spot in the grocery game. In China it
has forty-two stores in twenty cities.

Thanks to liberalization of foreign investment—part of China's
ticket into the World Trade Organization—Wal-Mart is now free to
open stores without having to partner with a Chinese company. With
the world's fastest-growing economy and middle class, China has the
potential, Wal-Mart executives have said, to house three thousand
Supercenters, more than the total the company sees for the United
States.[12] By the time you read this, Wal-Mart will have likely announced plans to open up in Russia, while keeping a close eye on
India as its next piece of intercontinental booty.

Wal-Mart has stated that its goal is to have its International
Division account for approximately 30 percent of the company's
overall annual sales. In 2004, it was holding at 18 percent, up from
only 8.9 five years earlier. Despite slow growth in Germany and
rocky starts in South America, there's little reason to believe it won't
meet its goal, if not surpass it entirely.

While Wal-Mart has ambitious designs on reaching the global
market, it has already, like many American companies, been rubbing
the seamy underbelly of Third World labor markets, including areas
where an "able and willing employee" is underpaid, underfed, and,
sometimes, under age ten. Wal-Mart's missteps in its use of Third
World labor have become legendary—the name Kathie Lee is enough
to conjure images of a tearful television sprite claiming innocence,
intercut with video of disgusting sweatshops filled with children
stitching casual wear. While Wal-Mart was not the only big com-

pany to take heat on the issue of child labor and sweatshops in the nineties, its public blunders were certainly more memorable than those involving Nike or Gap.

The first official media nightmare for Wal-Mart aired on *Dateline NBC,* in 1993, less than a year after Sam Walton's death. Viewed by more than fourteen million people, the segment showed reporter Brian Ross confronting Wal-Mart CEO David Glass with apparel found in more than ten Wal-Mart stores, shelved beneath MADE IN THE USA signs. The clothing had been made in Bangladesh.

At the time, Wal-Mart was touring its "Buy American" program, a pet project of Sam Walton's that had been conceived in the mid-eighties, when more and more manufacturing jobs were heading overseas. It had been designed to win the hearts and dollars of consumer patriots in areas of the country where jobs had been disappearing, replaced with a new virulent strain of economic nationalism. Walton boasted of favoring domestic manufacturers and garnered a considerable amount of positive media coverage due to several well-publicized contracts with domestic companies producing metal fans, garden chairs, and men's dress shirts.[13]

However, the company's less-publicized rider to those contracts made the concept of "American-made" one that would cause even the most brittle postmodernist to scratch his or her head. Domestic suppliers had to meet the prices of overseas competitors, something generally considered impossible given the prevailing wages in Asia and Central America. And if the suppliers couldn't quite make it, then Wal-Mart would either terminate the contract or step in and make bulk purchases of material from overseas companies itself. This is exactly what happened with Farris Fashions.

One of the larger contracts Wal-Mart awarded under the Buy American program was with the Brinkley, Arkansas–based manufacturer of work shirts and athletic shorts. When Sam Walton phoned company president Farris Burroughs to express interest, Burroughs thought it was a joke, especially since Walton was calling from inside the governor's mansion, occupied at the time by Bill Clinton.[14] The contract to supply Wal-Mart with work shirts and gym shorts turned Farris from a tiny outfit of twenty workers to one employing nearly 500. But the only way it was able to hit an acceptably low "Wal-Mart" price was for Wal-Mart to intervene and purchase two million yards of material from a Taiwanese supplier.[15]

"There was not a domestic cotton maker that would even talk to us," Burroughs recalled in a 2004 interview.[16] But there were plenty of foreign cotton makers that would talk to Wal-Mart.

In the 1993 *Dateline* segment in which Brian Ross confronted Glass with Bangladeshi-made apparel, the CEO stumbled, then stuttered about how the apparel Ross handed him must have been mistakenly placed under the MADE IN THE USA banners. Ross then asked Glass to watch a few scenes from a video showing Wal-Mart apparel being stitched by children in a Bangladeshi factory. Glass watched, unmoved. He said it proved nothing. Ross tried again: he handed Glass photographs taken inside the Bangladeshi factory after a fire in which twenty-five child workers had been killed just a year before Wal-Mart's contractors set up shop there.[17]

"There are tragic things that happen all over the world," Glass responded after looking at the photographs. As if on cue, Wal-Mart's vice president of corporate affairs, Don Shinkle, entered stage right and, with the cameras still rolling, declared the interview over.

As author Bob Ortega notes, a second interview was arranged after Glass whined—to Jack Welch, the CEO of NBC's parent company, General Electric, and a longtime admirer of Sam Walton—about being ambushed. Despite the second chance, though, Glass came off no better. When asked about the alleged use of child labor in Wal-Mart–contracted factories overseas, Glass said, "You and I might, perhaps, define children differently." He also noted that it was often tough to discern the age of Asians, as they're quite short.[18]

The *Dateline* episode generated more audience reaction than any of its segments to date. Much of it came from Wal-Mart employees who felt the piece was a hatchet job. Rushing to defend itself, Wal-Mart encouraged more than one hundred of its suppliers, including GE, to take out full-page sympathy ads in major newspapers.[19] At that point, though, it was too little too late. Glass's on-air intransigence helped cement the idea that Wal-Mart was exactly the sort of Dickensian corporation that had no qualms about profiting from child labor.

KATHIE LEE: *E! TRUE HOLLYWOOD STORY* OR WAL-MART FALL GAL?

Four years after the *Dateline* debacle, Wal-Mart was again bent over and buggered in the press, though this time there was a celebrity stand-in to take the hit. Her name: Kathie Lee Gifford.

As a response to Kmart's enormously successful Jaclyn Smith line of women's clothing, Wal-Mart launched its own Kathie Lee brand in 1995.

Now just one more *E! True Hollywood Story,* Gifford was a big deal in the mid-nineties. Married to football star turned sports announcer Frank Gifford, Kathie Lee had worked her way through game shows and daytime dramas and was the perky-to-the-point-of-nauseating cohost of ABC's *Live with Regis and Kathie Lee* morning show.

Gifford fancied herself a children's advocate, donating 10 percent of the proceeds from her clothing line to children's charities. So it was a media moment too juicy to resist when the National Labor

Committee's Charles Kernigan went public with news that her apparel was stitched in Honduras by teenage girls making thirty cents an hour.

While stories of overseas sweatshops had come across the wires before, the passage of trade agreements like NAFTA and GATT had mobilized new coalitions of environmental and labor groups. Couple this with a vulnerable celebrity, and the media couldn't swill the story down fast enough, especially when Gifford was dissolving into unscripted, tearful histrionics on the air.

"You can say I'm ugly, you can say I'm not talented, but when you say I don't care about children and that I will exploit them for some sort of monetary gain . . . how *dare* you."

The sweatshop story didn't blow over. Neither did the Gifford saga; only a few weeks after the first story broke, another erupted within a few blocks of Gifford's New York television studios. The sweatshop in question had been making 50,000 Kathie Lee blouses for Wal-Mart, and owed hundreds in back pay to workers who had been making less than minimum wage with no overtime. In a hurry to do the right thing or run damage control, Frank Gifford passed out envelopes, each stuffed with $300 in cash, to angry workers assembled at the Garment District Justice Center.[20]

Wal-Mart eventually reimbursed Gifford, ceased doing business with the contractor, and left the fracas in much better shape than Kathie Lee Gifford had. Although Wal-Mart renewed its contract on the Kathie Lee line, it phased it out over the next five years, eliminating it entirely by 2003.

Many companies, learning from Wal-Mart's mistakes, were quick to adopt corporate codes of conduct; Gap, in particular, allowed limited inspections of its factories by independent organizations. It's a move that Wal-Mart, however, has never been willing to make.

PROCEEDS FROM THE SALE OF THIS ITEM HELP MOVE JOBS TO GUANGDONG! WAL-MART GOES GLOBAL

Over the past decade, the curtain concealing Wal-Mart's corporate activities has been yanked back countless times, exposing its questionable labor practices, its corrosive effect on local economies, its bullying of suppliers, its growing reliance on foreign outfits, and its growing political muscle. But the wizards behind Bentonville's curtain, unlike the one from Oz, show no shame when their true actions are revealed. Rather, they're emboldened beyond measure, and they're very, very busy.

But still, illusion is important, and there's no good in upsetting anybody if you can avoid it, so the "curtain"—a slick commercial featuring a sympathetic single mom, an underwriter's announcement on NPR, a well-placed ad appearing in a newspaper in a battle-ground community—has its uses.

Lee Scott takes care to note that Wal-Mart has only "nine percent" of the domestic retail market. He also suggests that few of his 136 million weekly customers give a crap that Wal-Mart is the world's largest retailer. And he's right. But there are some people who do care about this distinction, and about its implications. Maybe you know some of them: they're people who used to have jobs.

PILLOWTEX

In July of 2003, nearly 5,000 Pillowtex workers lost their jobs—in North Carolina alone. The Dallas-based textile giant had been facing mounting losses due, its executives said, to globalization. The closing of the Kannapolis, North Carolina, factory devastated the Charlotte region.

After years of supplying Wal-Mart with towels, the pressure to keep prices down became unmanageable for Pillowtex, but working with another discounter was out of the question; in its final years the retailer made up 30 percent of Pillowtex's total business. As former chairman Chuck Hansen told CNBC, "Price became more and more of the driving object, and more and more suggestions were made [like], 'Well, if you can't make it in the United States, why don't you make it offshore?'"

By way of anecdote, Hansen relayed a private conversation he said he had with David Glass. "I asked him—there were some other gentlemen present—and I said, 'Could you describe Wal-Mart to me? How do you envision Wal-Mart?' He said, 'I envision Wal-Mart as a speeding truck that just wants to hit something.'"[1] (Glass would later deny making this comment.)

Pillowtex workers were hardly the labor aristocrats of Tom Wolfe's imagination. At the time of the last layoffs in Kannapolis, the average Pillowtex worker was forty-six years old and earning $22,610 a year. Nearly 50 of workers percent had not completed high school. Most had been rooted in the area for generations, building families, buying homes, and living on the fringe of the middle class. A year after the plant's closing in 2003, more than a third of its workers were still unemployed, many getting by without health insurance. Cars have been repossessed, families have lost their homes, and alcohol abuse and domestic violence are on the rise.

Lee Scott publicly denies that Wal-Mart had anything to do with Pillowtex's demise. But Wal-Mart has also denied playing any role in the movement of American jobs overseas. Just as it boasts of passing on savings to consumers, the company shifts its social responsibility to them. It's as if every item sold at a Wal-Mart carried a consumer advisory label reading: "Proceeds from the sale of this item help move jobs to Guangdong!" It's as if it's the consumer's fault that everyone in Kannapolis is cashing unemployment checks. And maybe it is.

FROM UNDERDOG TO "TEMPLATE INDUSTRY"

Wal-Mart used to revel in its underdog status. It emphasized and reemphasized a you-and-me-against-the-world ethos that suggested that other retailers were price-gougers. Trust only Wal-Mart, 'cause we're just like you—tryin' to get by! In stores, managers set up displays of shopping carts filled to the brim with goods to underscore just how much lower its prices were than competitors'. But now that it's number one by a margin that renders the rearview mirror largely unnecessary, Wal-Mart has stopped setting up these sorts of displays. As Lee Scott concedes, "Now it just seems like we're rubbing it in."

Wal-Mart has become a model of what University of California–Santa Barbara professor Nelson Lichtenstein calls "a template industry," a company whose practices set the tone—and the bar—for a generation of business leaders. This is one reason why it's impossible to understand Wal-Mart in a vacuum. Confining the discussion to Bentonville's behavior is like trying to understand a presidential election without considering the state of the economy, the media, or the tenor of world politics. "Wal-Martization" is a phenomenon that transcends the concepts of retailing or manufacturing.

Wal-Mart is the muscle and sometimes the model behind one of the most excruciating changes in the last fifty years: globalization. The siphoning of well paid manufacturing jobs from "industrialized" countries like the United States, England, and Japan, to Mexico, China, and other developing nations has created a kind of paranoia, not just in towns reliant upon mills and factories, but also in white-collar enclaves where fears of outsourcing were once almost unheard of. North Carolina textile workers who grew up with little reason to doubt that the mill that employed their grandparents would see them to retirement find themselves waiting in line to pick up unemployment checks. The IBM programmer in exclusive Armonk, New York, who has a computer science degree and is halfway through a master's never dreamed he'd one day be competing with educated men and women on another continent—men and women willing to work for a fifth of his salary.

Wal-Martization is a movement whose cost-pinching values may result in a Texas cashier's pissing herself for want of a break,[2] and southeastern Chinese factory workers' pulling eighteen-hour shifts for pennies an hour. As a result, prices no longer fall to a place where they bottom out; rather, they're sucked into a deflationary vortex where few other businesses can follow without perishing.

And yet, in some camps, the Wal-Mart economy is a cause célèbre.

Some actually believe the company has single-handedly kept down the rate of inflation. In the nineties, when all eyes were on Silicon Valley and its hyperbolized rock-star CEOs, a McKinsey report concluded the *real* source of productivity gains came from . . . guess who?

The growth industry of pseudopopulism insists that Wal-Mart's low prices return dollars to working-class families. This, they assure us, frees up money that, in turn, creates jobs. (What *kind* of jobs they never say.) Investment guru Warren Buffett has called it the single greatest asset for poor people in America. According to *New York Times* columnist Thomas Friedman, the call centers of Bangalore, where young Indian men and women assume fake identities and undergo "accent neutralization" training, are examples only of the "outsourcing of geopolitics" and are full of "dignity and hope."[3] And the Cato Institute's Doug Bandow credits the privately run factories of southern China—with ambiguous labor standards and virtually no human-rights monitoring—as "the most powerful force for change in China."[4]

SURVEY SAYS . . . WE'RE FUCKED!

There are certainly positive aspects to Wal-Martization. As maddening as Thomas Friedman's patronizing corporate boosterism is, what kind of killjoy doesn't want poor people to have better jobs? Unfortunately, the people who trumpet the benefits of these jobs get high off productivity gains, inflation defense, and glib declarations that "the consumers have voted"; what is left unsaid—because it complicates things—is that Wal-Mart's continued rise coincides with the broomstick beating that working-class Americans are suffering.

In April 2000, the stock market's tech-bubble burst was followed by a slow recession that sprinted south after September 11.

When signs of life emerged in late 2001, it took so long for the effects to be felt in any appreciable way that economists began using the term "jobless recovery." In July of 2004, total payroll employment was 1.2 million less than it had been at the beginning of the recovery. If job growth had simply kept pace with population, four million more jobs would have been added.[5]

CHINA AND WAL-MART

So if an 800-pound gorilla can sit anywhere he wants at a dinner party, how does he behave when he's free of the constraints of polite society? If Wal-Mart is the gorilla, China is the jungle where cheap labor and government-funded infrastructure abound in almost limitless supply. No nation is as essential to Wal-Mart's global designs. No free press, no independent labor unions, no pesky human-rights organizations poking around factories, an almost eerie political stability—it's a retail giant's wet dream.

In 2004, Wal-Mart imported $15 billion worth of Chinese goods, up $3 billion from just a year earlier.[6] Continued trade liberalization and a massive internal migration from remote peasant villages into cities are the twin engines that have helped turn China into the world's fastest-growing economy.*

U.S. companies can find even cheaper labor in places like Myanmar, Haiti, or Bangladesh, and geography will always be on Mexico's side when it comes to goods bound for the United States. But China provides a combination of political stability, sturdy infrastructure,

---

*Calling it the greatest migration in human history, Ted Fishman of the *New York Times* estimates that the population of displaced Chinese peasants searching for work exceeds the entire working population of the United States.

and labor force willing to work for pennies an hour. Factory conditions go unmonitored by government agencies. Minimum wages are set by regional governments but are rarely enforced. In a Ching Hai factory, for example, that makes small appliances like toasters and juicers, workers are paid $32 a month—40 percent below the province's local minimum wage.[7]

But for many—and this is what both China and Wal-Mart rely on—the wages, meager as they are, represent a huge step up from life in the rural villages. Workers can often earn more than three times what they might subsist on at home.[8]

A report issued by the National Labor Committee (U.S.), one of the leading human-rights organizations investigating overseas sweatshops, paints a feudal scene. In the Qin Shi factory that makes leather goods for Wal-Mart, nearly half of its 800-employee workforce were making no wages at all. Instead, they toiled fourteen hours a day, seven days a week, to pay off a series of debts—for training, food, and lodging.

Wal-flacks insist the company routinely sends its own inspectors to the Chinese factories it contracts with; those found using child labor, engaging in forced overtime, or committing any other violation of local labor law will find their contracts terminated.

But the same National Labor Committee study of the Qin Shi factory found that Wal-Mart's inspections were telegraphed days in advance. In preparation for the visit, the workforce was divided in two, with half the workers continuing their Wal-Mart work and the other half pretending to be employees of a fictional company called the Yecheng Leather Parts Factory.

In addition, Wal-Mart refused to make public the names of its Chinese production facilities, estimated to total over 4,500.[9] Wal-Mart says its lips are sealed for "competitive reasons." Moreover, the company uses only its own hired inspectors. Labor activists claim the inspectors, in notifying the factories of their visits days in advance, gave them time to clean up the restrooms, adjust the paperwork, and tell their workers what to say. When it comes to disclosure, Wal-Mart stands in stark contrast to the Gap, which under intense public pressure in the late 1990s agreed to allow independent human-rights monitors inspect its overseas factories. In May 2004 it released its "social responsibility report," which contained much unflattering information about the state of its 3,000 global production facilities, 16 percent of which are in China.[10]

One of the results of the uproar over sweatshops in the 1990s was the creation of those corporate codes of conduct by retailers such as Nike, Gap, and Liz Claiborne. Wal-Mart was one of many to craft such documents, but because there's virtually no independent monitoring of its Chinese factories, it's been impossible to assess the effects of its codes. One Chinese manufacturer told the *Wall Street Journal* that he did not do business with companies with codes of conduct; they were, he said, "inconvenient." Buyers weren't hard to come by, he noted. What was truly eating his lunch was the need to meet price demands and still eke out a profit.[11]

Chinese government officials and manufacturers claim the codes limit business, as well as the labor supply, since peasant workers, they say, don't consider it worth their while to ship out from the countryside when the codes cap working hours and overtime.[12]

OUTSOURCING: AN UNEASY CONSENSUS

Losing a $50,000-a-year gig[13] with health benefits may suck, but fear not: the global economy has your back. You'll get another job soon. Such "headcount rationalizations" lower costs, deliver increases in productivity, and permit investment in ways that will surely, inevitably, and completely mysteriously create more jobs. Exactly when these new jobs will come, who will qualify for them, and under what circumstances is rarely specified. Neither is the industrial flavor of the oft-prescribed "training." Nevertheless, free-market ideologues still surfing the withering crest of the halcyon days of irrational exuberance insist that such trade practices are sure to benefit America as a whole.

Lest they concede to cracks in the design, the bipartisan cheerleaders create an imaginary class of consumers whose needs are so distinct from those of workers one wonders if they even breathe the same air. *Houston Chronicle* business columnist Loren Steffy claims increased productivity is entirely driven by this alien class, who choose Wal-Mart's prices over the local hardware store in an almost subconscious vote for outsourcing. Trade barriers of any sort will only hurt a nation of incurable discount addicts: "The people making lower wages now have to pay more for shoes at Wal-Mart because Wal-Mart can't import cheaper shoes from China."[14]

This is not to discredit all of globalization's rationale: American college and graduate students are about as interested in fields like engineering and computer science as they are in blacksmithing and barrel-staving. Combined with the aging of the American population, this apathy will create a shortage of American workers in high-tech fields. But as recent trends have shown, these are not the only jobs in jeopardy. Almost any occupation hinging on a computer and a modem is up for grabs.

In an essay published in the *Journal of Economic Perspectives*,* Nobel Prize–winning economist Paul A. Samuelson challenged what

*Paul A. Samuelson, "Where Ricardo and Mill Rebut and Confirm Arguments of Mainstream Economists Supporting Globalization," *Journal of Economic Perspectives* 18, 3 (Summer 2004), pp. 135–46.

he calls "the popular polemical untruth" that globalization is inherently good for the U.S. economy. Arguing against some of his former students, including the chairman of the White House Council of Economic Advisers, Gregory Mankiwitz, renowned economist Jagdish N. Bhagwati, and Fed lifer Alan Greenspan, Samuelson disputed the consensus that globalization is inherently beneficial for the American worker. "Being able to purchase groceries 20 percent cheaper at Wal-Mart," he told the *New York Times,* "does not necessarily make up for the wage losses."[15]

THE CONSUMER MADE ME DO IT!

In a softball interview typical of the kind Lee Scott agrees to, CNBC's David Faber asked the Wal-Mart don about the company's role in offshoring. Scott answered, "Moving offshore started a long time before we got to be the largest sales company in the world. . . ." Asked whether or not Wal-Mart hastened the process, Scott responded, "No, I don't think so. I think you get into a lot of trouble when you assume that anybody who asks for efficiencies somehow causes bad things to occur, because what are you going to do, set a standard that you should say—you should bring your supplier in and say, 'We'd like to pay you 50 cents more per item so that you can do all this good in the world' or whatever? I mean, we're the customers' agent. The idea is that we say—we sit down with you and say, 'How do we take cost out of doing business with you?'"[16]

A company with a mandate for "taking cost out of doing business" is working with a whole different set of standards and goals than past giants of American retail. Whereas other retailers—indeed, any other business in America—accepts the fact that cost is an unavoidable element of doing business, Wal-Mart seems engaged in a near-maniacal quest to create costless profit. With this kind of ethos—the kind Scott professed to in the CNBC interview and dozens more—it's no wonder that jobs are flying overseas, that Wal-Mart's domestic workers are getting paid below the wage that many communities consider to be "livable," and that suppliers like Pillow-tex are folding under the pressure.

But jobs aren't the only things Wal-Mart is outsourcing; as the press gets worse and worse, it has taken to outsourcing its responsi-bility to the consumers, who, after all, are the ones who want low prices in the first place.[17]

Of course, it would be a fantasy to think a can of "Wal-Mart-B-Gon" would single-handedly reverse the flight of manufacturing jobs overseas. Even within the loosely knit antiglobalization movement there's a growing recognition that this is not likely to happen. As Barbara Briggs of the National Labor Committee observes, "Can we stop globalization? Can we reestablish borders and start produc-ing stuff here in the U.S.? There's increasing clarity that this is not going to happen, that going back to a non-globalized economy is not realistic."

That's why Briggs and others have worked for more than a decade to bring home the human face behind our products. Arrang-ing for workers from Honduras and Bangladesh to tour America and tell their stories about factory conditions has helped increase the awareness of the problem, even if definitive solutions haven't exactly made themselves evident.

The idea posited by Wal-Mart and its friends is that consumers consciously vote manufacturing jobs offshore every time they buy a foreign-made product—or, in the words of Wal-Mart's Michael Duke, "choose quality." But where exactly is the choice? Does Wal-Mart make a point of educating consumers about its suppliers and the provenance of its products? Should it be required to do so? Has it ever agreed to disclose the names and locations of its facilities or, just for kicks, let an independent human-rights monitor inspect its contracted factories? What about providing "fair trade" alternatives for products on its shelves? It sounds like a pipe dream, but if Wal-Mart is as committed to "the consumer" as it claims to be, why not offer a real choice? Maybe the consumer doesn't care. But the blame has been shifted, and it's now on the shoulders of every shopper who enters Wal-Mart: You're the bad guy.

PART TWO

THE UNITED STATES OF WAL-MART

Kenneth H. Cleaver
P.O. Box 810
Bedford, NY 10506

June 15, 2003

Mr. Tom Williams
Spokesman
Wal-Mart Stores Inc.
702 Southwest 8th Street
Bentonville, Arkansas 72716

Dear Mr. Williams:

I was saddened to learn that Wal-Mart will no longer carry Maxim, Stuff and FHM (For Him Magazine). I understand you fancy yourself a "family store" and that publications featuring barely dressed, barely legal women have been deemed inappropriate.

You do realize that the women featured in these magazines are not mere models: Many have appeared on such acclaimed documentary television programs as Temptation Island and The Bachelor.

Usually once a month my son and I make a Wal-Mart run for dried foods, paper towels, and the odd power tool. But our favorite part, hands down, is the magazine rack. After browsing a few lesser titles — Field & Stream, Soldier of Fortune, American Conservative — I usually pick up the latest Maxim and Stuff for me and the boy.

While these publications might not be appropriate for every family, they have taught my son and I a great deal about the career trajectories of pop stars. We've also gotten a chance to see a wide variety of really hot women. But more than that, the service pieces and columns have broadened our perspectives on sex and love.

Take, for example, the extensive reporting on how to ensure that new communication technologies do not interfere with clandestine romantic conquests. Also illuminating is the advice to seek out "hotties" in places where they are most vulnerable: emergency rooms, bail bond agencies, and funeral homes.

I am always finding these magazines scattered around my boy's bedside and closet. I know that he will be a reader for life and that it will remain something we will share for years to come. While we can still purchase these magazines at other venues, I am disappointed that we do not fit into your definition of family.

Sincerely,

Kenneth Cleaver

Kenneth Cleaver

WAL★MART

WAL-MART STORES, INC.
CORPORATE OFFICES
702 S.W. 8TH STREET
BENTONVILLE, AR 72716
PHONE (479) 277-3195
FAX (479) 273-1970

June 30, 2003

Mr. Kenneth Cleaver
P. O. Box 810
Bedford, NY 10506

Dear Mr. Cleaver:

Thank you for taking the time to share your opinion regarding the magazines that we offer in our stores.

Even though customer demand led us to initially offer the magazines Maxim, Stuff and FHM, we have had customers around the country that have consistently made us aware that they are uncomfortable with us carrying these selections. In this case we had to balance the interests of two different customer sets, and we made the decision to stop selling these magazines. It was a judgement call on our part.

Serving the one hundred million customers who shop in our stores each week can be quite challenging, yet it is something we have been committed to do for more than 40 years. Again, thank you for sharing your concern with us. We always appreciate hearing from our customers.

Sincerely,

B. Brown dkh

Barbara Brown
Vice-President, Customer Service/Operations

SEVEN

SPIN CITY

Over the years, we have thought that we could sit in
Bentonville, take care of our customers, take care
of associates and the world would leave us alone.
It just does not work that way anymore.

—WAL-MART CEO LEE SCOTT[1]

On the very first page of his memoir, Sam Walton took aim
at the invasive hordes of media swooping down upon the
innocent hamlet of Bentonville with hopes of finding him
living the high life of a merchant prince. They never succeeded.

It's an interesting point of view coming from a guy who owed his
early meals to newspapers: from the time he was eleven until he left
Missouri to become a J. C. Penney trainee a few years later, Walton
had been a newspaper man. As a kid, it was just a paper route, and
the odd campaign to push magazine subscriptions. In college, deliv-
ering the *Columbia Missourian* financed his entire education. Later in
life, newspapers would keep Walton abreast of the goings-on in the
larger business world, a place he rarely visited from his isolated

pocket of Arkansas. And yet, when he was in the news, Walton saw nothing but infestation.

Around the mid-1980s, Wal-Mart became saddled with a designation that it still wears today: the preeminent assassin of small businesses. *Time,* the *Wall Street Journal,* the *New York Times,* and countless smaller newspapers jumped on the story, running headlines like: ARRIVAL OF DISCOUNTER TEARS THE CIVIC FABRIC OF SMALL-TOWN LIFE;[2] WHEN WAL-MART COMES TO TOWN; and THE TWO SIDES OF THE SAM WALTON LEGACY.[3] The articles were depressing, often focusing on small communities that were reeling from the arrival of a Wal-Mart. Sensing a classic David-and-Goliath narrative in the making, the media latched on to the story, each outlet seeking its own specific example of a Wal-Mart casualty.

In 1989, the *New York Times Magazine* profiled the small town of Independence, Iowa, in a cover story. A year after Wal-Mart set up shop there, a dozen downtown businesses—some of them local institutions active for a century or more—shut their doors for good. As one embittered, chain-smoking proprietor put it, "We can't compete against the richest-man-in-the-world's prices. You just try to do the best you can and hang on to your loyal customers by providing service."[4] *Time* traveled to Albany, Missouri, where it eulogized a small hardware store owned by James and Richard McConkey. In 1985 their store was pummeled by two Wal-Marts in nearby towns to the east and west.

"Their parking lots were full of McConkey's neighbors and friends," the article read, "lured there through the winter's cold by the powerful Wal-Mart merchandising mystique and retail prices often below his wholesale cost.[5]

The *Wall Street Journal* found a similar scene in another heartland town, Pawhuska, Oklahoma, but one that signaled the possibility of communities choosing to fight back. Several Pawhuska merchants were involved in a lawsuit that charged the giant retailer under a seldom-invoked state law prohibiting stores from selling below cost. Wal-Mart would eventually prevail in the suit, spending thousands on lobbyists and advertisements encouraging customers in the region to stand up against high prices. Wal-Mart's campaign created bitterness and resentment among the town's retailers, as they faced routine accusations of price-gouging from their dwindling pool of customers.

In his memoirs, Walton seemed befuddled by the idea that his company had an adverse impact on small merchants. His response remains the stock line Wal-flacks parrot today: downtowns were declining before Wal-Mart came along. The proliferation of automobiles, interstate highways, and the rise of supermarkets and shopping centers acclimated people to the idea of traveling by car to shop.

Walton attributed the criticism lobbed at his company to two things: the sentimentality of urbanites and the media's hunger for "story." The former he chalked up to city people pining for a way of life that no longer existed. "Somehow, small-town populations weren't supposed to move out into their own suburbs, and they weren't supposed to go out to the intersections of highways and build malls with lots of free parking," Walton wrote. "That's just not the way some of these people remember their old towns."[6]

The media, on the other hand, were the same nattering nabobs of negativism Spiro Agnew complained of, an institution profoundly disinterested in aspirations, delighting instead in your failures and reflexively suspicious of success. "If you ever become a large scale success, it's Katie bar the door. Suddenly you become a very convenient villain because everybody seems to love shooting at who's on top."[7]

But if Walton were still alive today, he might be surprised to find just how many of the vermin actually take his side. In addition to certain pundits and assorted op-ed rock stars, Wal-Mart's cast of boosters includes a mishmash of free-market cheerleaders, conservative contrarians, and pseudopopulists. And they're entirely right in some of their main assertions. Wal-Mart's low prices likely save the American consumer millions each year. Paramount in the arsenal of pro–Wal-Mart tautologies, however, is the most obvious: No one is forced to shop there. And yet people do. Despite a litany of bad press and surveys showing mixed feelings even among its customers, over 100 million people put money in its coffers each week. Even the United Food and Commercial Workers Union, an organization with as vested an interest as any in stemming Wal-Mart's tide, has confessed it can't keep its own members out of the stores.

"The main reason we can't shop at Ed's Variety Store anymore," writes *Fortune* magazine's Jerry Useem, "is that we stopped shopping at Ed's Variety Store."

Pithy, sure, but completely accurate? As Wal-Mart's growth machine plunders on, regional grocery stores bite the dust at a ratio of two to every new Supercenter. Fearing a fight they can't win, competing national chains like Albertsons and Publix have packed up from entire markets shortly after Wal-Mart's arrival.* People who never chose to shop at Wal-Mart in the first place now have one less place to go.

But Bentonville's apologists herald the Wal-Mart–bound consumer stampede as an unassailable referendum on its merits. As George Will writes in *Newsweek,* "The tone and tactics of the war against Wal-Mart suggest that it is colored, as is much of today's politics, by the contempt of 'progressives' for what they consider the vulgarity of popular tastes."[8]

"I hope it's not too McCarthyite to suggest that those who dis-

---

*In 2001, the Boise-based Albertsons, the nation's fourth-largest grocery retailer, ceded the Houston area in the face of Wal-Mart's rapid expansion.

like Wal-Mart are those who may not be so crazy about America *tout court*."⁹ That charmer is from the *National Review's* Jay Nordlinger. Other right-wing scolds are only too delighted to smear opponents an even deeper shade of Jane Fonda. In Ann Coulter's resident outlet *Human Events,* Luke Boggs doffs the condom of nuance: "Wal-Mart is unreservedly patriotic. Liberal elites are not."¹⁰

Criticize Wal-Mart and you're guilty of a host of socio-ideological sins ranging from special-interest pandering to downright anti-Americanism. Point out its low wages and meager benefits and you're the butt boy of organized labor. Say that it's bad for independent businesses and you're a hopelessly sentimental alarmist or, worse still, an enemy of competition—and thus of capitalism itself.

Through the media, the Wal-Mart story has become increasingly politicized. Following the logic of "the enemy of my enemy is my friend," the right-wing press corps has appointed itself as the company's reasoned defender. In the diverse spectrum of Wal-Mart's opposition they manage to see a unified chorus of a reflexively anticapitalist left. Leading the frothing mob is the house organ of liberal orthodoxy, also known as the *New York Times.* In *National Review,* Nordlinger highlights some of the Gray Lady's critical coverage before claiming that Wal-Mart has done McDonald's "this favor: It has replaced the hamburger chain as Bogeyman No. 1 in the mind and rhetoric of the Left." Never mind that the House of Kroc hasn't been the subject of a *Nation* editorial for well over a decade; Nordlinger's suggestion is that the critique of Wal-Mart is purely a partisan affair. It's a cute idea, bolstered by a string of potshots made by Democratic presidential hopefuls on the '04 the primary trail. And squeezing Wal-Mart into the master narrative of red state versus blue makes for a timely analogy, but falls short of a real analysis.

The truth is considerably more complicated, and, arguably, it's

fueling Wal-Mart's own media rethink more than any series of articles "the left" might scribble. In recent years, pinko-commie organs
like *Fortune, Forbes, Fast Company, The Economist,* and the *Wall Street
Journal,* to name a few, have all written very critically on Wal-Mart.
The tone might not be as strident as in the *Progressive* or *Mother Jones,*
but the analysis shares a common theme: Power doesn't come without consequence, and low prices are neither a panacea nor a passport
to the problems they create.

The Economist frets that Wal-Mart's turnover problem may force
the company to increase its labor costs, and that signs indicate that
its price deflation is starting to slow. *BusinessWeek* points out that its
"cultural gate keeping" practices like censoring racy music and magazines don't reflect the values of its new constituencies in places like
Los Angeles.

The criticism doesn't end with the business glossies. *Workforce
Management,* a trade publication for HR professionals, slammed Wal-
Mart for its labor practices, suggesting that some of its troubles stem
from seeing HR as little more than a cost generator. *Advertising Age*
has critiqued Wal-Mart's stance on magazine censorship. *Computer-
world* kvetches about how its demand for expensive radio frequency
identification tags will cost suppliers and save Wal-Mart billions,
but offer scant returns for suppliers.

Geography plays a unique role in the Wal-Mart news blitz.
Business stories often concern the malfeasance of top executives
within a particular company. When the stories go national, they're
generally dominated by the largest outlets, which can afford to "flood
the zone," in Howell Raines's famous phrase, with teams of reporters.
Ground zero for these stories is usually one of two places: the company's
hometown or the site of the federal courthouse where charges were
filed. Wal-Mart offers the media an alternative scenario: whether the

outrage du jour is gender discrimination, opposition from neighbors, or a union-organizing drive, a local angle is only a store away.

OUR PACS MAKE THE DIFFERENCE

In its relationship to the political world, Wal-Mart has veered from the abstinence position dictated by Sam Walton and David Glass to that of noted player. Between 2000 and 2003, the company went from political nonentity to the second-largest corporate PAC. Though that designation was overshadowed during the 2004 elections, the company gave more money to President Bush and other Republican candidates than to Democrats by a factor of four to one. As Wal-Mart's communication vice president Jay Allen has said, "We needed to engage at this level by donating to candidates who share the company's priorities."[11]

Like Microsoft in the mid-nineties, which boasted, via Bill Gates, that it was from "the other Washington" and then proceeded to shower Capitol Hill with antitrust lobbyists and dollars, Wal-Mart has become a presence inside the Beltway. In 1999, then Senate majority leader Trent Lott traveled to Bentonville to coach management on how to "play the Washington game." Jay Allen told the *Financial Times* that "a need frankly still exists today, with everything that is going on, for people to understand us better. When you are not there it creates a void that someone else is going to fill, and you may not like their definition of you."[12] So far, Wal-Mart has thrown its weight around by lobbying for restrictions aimed at keeping unions at bay (surprise, surprise) and for reduced taxes on offshore operations, but has homed in mainly on the question of trade restrictions. When you're importing $15 billion worth of goods from China alone, you don't want to get bitten in the ass because you're too busy making sure your customers "understand you better."

So when you've become a poster child for the country's most structurally embedded ills, what's a behemoth to do, especially as the march of time finds that the old charges don't disappear while new dirt arrives all the time? The answer, of course, is to buy friends, influence people, and spin, spin, spin.

OUR PROPAGANDA
MAKES THE DIFFERENCE

A middle-aged African-American woman from the Baldwin Hills section of South Central Los Angeles wants you to know she's *thrilled* with the good life at Wal-Mart: the opportunities for advancement, the benefits, the people. Heck, she even encouraged her own daughter to join the "Wal-Mart family." In a neighborhood famously ravaged by the usual suspects of urban decline—the drug trade, gang violence, and chronic unemployment—Wal-Mart offers a ray of hope. And when a Wal-Mart sets up shop in an abandoned Macy's that had lain vacant for five years because neither Nordstrom, Ikea, nor any other retailer would touch it, well, that's when Wal-Mart became Buddha-like in its compassion.

Ms. Willie Cole tells you that Wal-Mart is good for women, that it's good for African-Americans, that it's good for cities.

"In this part of L.A.," she says in this Wal-Mart commercial, "our community has been overlooked by a lot of organizations. But when Wal-Mart came in, they let us know that they cared."

If Cole's story is not enough to knock the crust off your stale heart, consider, then, the case of John Millwood, an assistant manager at an east Texas Supercenter.

"I don't think people know how great the benefits are at Wal-Mart," he tells the camera in another Wal-Mart ad. Millwood's two-year-old son suffered from a rare form of liver cancer. A private jet, provided by Wal-Mart, transported the child to a treatment center in Minnesota, Millwood tells us. Wal-Mart covered his son's medical costs, which exceeded a million dollars. "Without Wal-Mart, he wouldn't—" Here he falters. "I don't know that he'd have made it. I don't know that *we* would have made it."

These are just two of the stories featured in Wal-Mart's "Good Jobs" ad campaign, the company's impressive, albeit tardy, attempt to polish its tarnished image. But if you know the story of Wal-Mart, these thirty-second video hybrids (part personal biography, part corporate paean), these exceptions to the rule, seem almost cruelly ironic.

At what point does "folksiness," become implausible? At $288 billion in annual sales, or over $10 billion in profit? Is it when a store's proximity to an ancient Aztec holy site is met with hunger strikes? Or is it when it becomes the second-largest political donor in the nation?

The power of carefully chosen language and tireless repetition can have its intended effect. Relying on egalitarian buzzwords and company cheers at shareholder meetings might seem laughable tactics to the high-minded. But such tactics work. Seeking the comfort of inclusion is as integral a part of human nature as is acting in your own self-interest. Wal-Mart panders to the former while its decision-makers adhere only to the latter.

WAL-FLACKS

Formally known as directors of corporate communications and public relations specialists, outside Bentonville they're simply Wal-flacks.

It's their job to paint a smiley face on a canvas of suck. The general in the forty-plus-strong army of Wal-flacks is one Mona Williams. Like Exxon's long-suffering PR guy Tom Cirigliano, Williams has a thankless job, but one that requires fluency in a language with its own unique vocabulary, syntax, and diction. For example, in defending the quality of Wal-Mart jobs to the *San Francisco Chronicle,* Williams said: "More than 40 percent of associates on our health care plan had no coverage at all before coming to Wal-Mart." Uhhh . . . yeah. And they probably didn't have a job before coming to Wal-Mart, either.

In restating the obvious and hoping it passes for reassuring logic, Wal-flacks help present the company not as the biggest corporation the world has ever seen, but as a sort of humanitarian relief agency. Media training was never part of the education process for the company's current crop of leaders, but Sam Walton did stress the idea that Wal-Mart wasn't all about the Benjamins. Rather, the message was this: by using its low-price strategy it was raising the living standards for the country as a whole.

When Lee Scott began making the media rounds in 2004, he expanded on this theme by stressing that many Wal-Mart customers are people who live paycheck to paycheck. Scott often notes that 20 percent of his customers do not even have a checking account.[13] One has to wonder at the selectiveness of Scott's concern. It's worth his while to trumpet the fact that Wal-Mart helps those living paycheck to paycheck, but absent from his self-congratulatory elocution is any mention of the hundreds of thousands of Wal-Mart associates who are also living paycheck to paycheck. If Wal-Mart is the balm for the low-income masses yearning to be free, then it is also the shackle that keeps the low-income masses chained to jobs like those at Wal-Mart.

But all of this, the Wal-flacks say, is just a misreading of the company's mission and a flat-out dismissal of all its good deeds. The company has simply failed to get its story out. Not everyone is buying this.

"Wal-Mart's response to this extensive list of labor problems," Representative George Miller wrote in his report from the U.S. House of Representatives' Committee on Education and the Workforce, "has been to treat the charges as a public-relations matter and not a substantive issue of workplace fairness. Seemingly, Wal-Mart believes only its image—not its behavior—needs to be adjusted."[14]

It might be hard for Wal-Mart to believe, but critical press is not always the result of bad or inadequate PR or an ideological agenda. Sometimes unflattering stories can actually come from unflattering facts.

EIGHT

IT'S A WAL-MART WORLD
AFTER ALL

Tens of thousands of foot soldiers dropped their weapons, grabbed their heads or their chests, fell to their knees, and writhed as they were invisibly sliced asunder. Their innards and entrails gushed to the desert floor, and as those around them turned to run, they too were slain, their blood pooling and rising in the unforgiving brightness of the glory of Christ."

These unfortunate souls are "seculars"—or nonbelievers—and in Dr. Timothy LaHaye's apocalyptic novel series Left Behind, they get their divine comeuppance.[1]

But LaHaye is no raving lunatic whose only audience resides in his own imagination. He's a best-selling author, a Wal-Mart favorite son, and a "prophetic Scholar" guy who can say, with complete honesty, that he's sold more than forty million copies of books with his name on the cover.

Some of those copies are in the hands of people waiting in line outside the Wal-Mart Supercenter in Bossier City, Louisiana. The crowd of mostly white, middle-aged folks is awaiting the arrival of the seventy-seven-year-old preacher and scholar who might be . . . who could be . . . the harbinger of the End Times, the ultimate final liquidation (that Wal-Mart will never have).

Dr. LaHaye's books are fictionalized riffs rooted in the Book of Revelation that read like pulp thrillers. They're conceived by Dr. LaHaye, an evangelical Christian, and written by Jerry B. Jenkins, a Christian novelist. The book that people are lining up to have Dr. LaHaye autograph today is *Glorious Appearing,* the series' twelfth and final installment, in which Christ makes his long-awaited return. And it's just in time, too, as a worldwide government (led by a Romanian Antichrist)—which goes by the name "United Nations"—has mutated into a savage dictatorship. As the end draws nigh, thousands of Jews are converted, while millions of "seculars," like the poor shlubs in the passage above, meet a gruesome death. Wal-Mart's definition of family-friendly may exclude Sheryl Crow and Jon Stewart, but descriptions of excruciatingly painful and violent deaths to non-Christians? What could bring a family closer?

There is, in fact, an interesting parallel between the plot of LaHaye's novel and the narrative of Wal-Mart itself. Who are the forcibly converted in Wal-Mart's apocalyptic world? Who is the Antichrist? And who are the decimated nonbelievers? If one were feeling creative, one could argue that, respectively, the tightly squeezed suppliers, the threat of regulation, and the smaller stores that go out of business when Wal-Mart comes into town fit the bill nicely. But as much as he might wish it were true, LaHaye's apocalypse is fiction; Wal-Mart's version, complete with "preachers," "believers," "converted," and the "damned," is no novel, and its story is not quite so clear-cut.

In the run-up to the book's release, Wal-Mart offered free first chapters of *Glorious Appearing* at thousands of its stores, so it was probably no surprise that Dr. LaHaye would pay a visit to his biggest corporate fan during his twelve-city Bible Belt book tour. Lee Scott, who describes the Left Behind series as "inspirational," notes that LaHaye's books have been among the company's biggest-sellers in recent years.*

Like Tim LaHaye, party girl and amateur pornstar Paris Hilton is signing copies of her own tome, *Confessions of an Heiress* (which, while milder than LaHaye's version of Judgment Day, might be considered equally apocalyptic), at a Santa Clarita, California, Wal-Mart. The crowd is younger than LaHaye's, as they seek news not of the rapture but of the "it" girl to end all "it" girls. Her Wal-Mart appearance is camp: on her reality TV show, *The Simple Life,* she was evidently the last person in America to learn of the retailer's existence. "What's Wal-Mart?" Hilton asked her heartland host family. "What, do they sell *wall* stuff?"

At a Wal-Mart in Wilmington, North Carolina, a crowd awaits emotion pornographer Nicholas Sparks. The author, whose physical appearance and demeanor were likened to that of a "Golf Channel announcer" by one local reporter,[2] is signing copies of *The Notebook*

---

*With the increasing popularity of Christian books, music, and videos, independent Christian merchants are now among the ranks of independent businesses feeling the Wal-Mart squeeze. According to *Forbes* magazine, Wal-Mart pulls in over $1 billion in Christian merchandise, roughly 25 percent of the whole U.S. market for such goods. In 2003, over 270 independent Christian stores went out of business. As one consultant glibly informed a trade-association workshop, "Ministry has to take a backseat to business acumen if success is going to happen." Interestingly, one of the advisors to the Christian Booksellers Association is former Wal-Mart executive Don Soderquist.

in conjunction with the release of its major motion picture adaptation, starring James Garner and Gena Rowlands. Wal-Mart trumpets the book as a "pick," stocking it in cardboard displays that plug both the book and the movie. (A Kleenex display is set up nearby for those of Sparks's admirers who are overcome.)

Has Wal-Mart become the nation's new literary arbiter? An egalitarian salon that hosts impassioned debates about high art in an unpretentious setting? Hardly. But the company is, with a restricted literary selection, beginning to shape America's literary sensibilities nonetheless.

A typical Wal-Mart carries only 500 titles, a fraction of the stock carried by most bookstores. The majority of these titles are bestsellers, airport-rack potboilers, and inspirational titles. Because of the company's sheer size, selling power, and access to consumers, every book publisher is desperate to nail the Wal-Mart/Sam's Club account, and the fear of alienating Bentonville that is palpable in the sales departments of publishing companies can doom projects that were never meant to be sold to the behemoth retailer in the first place.

The saga of a small San Francisco publisher, Jossey-Bass, provides a case in point. Jossey-Bass is a small imprint of John Wiley & Sons, a New Jersey–based publisher known for its schmaltzy but preposterously successful Chicken Soup for the Soul series. In 2003, Jossey-Bass editor Johanna Vondeling made an oral agreement to buy Greg LeRoy's book *The Great American Jobs Scam,* on the basis of the author's proposal. It was to be a collection of tales about things gone wrong when large corporations, such as Wal-Mart, receive public subsidies. The book was to have an entire chapter devoted to Wal-Mart.

With contracts drafted, but not yet signed, as Matt Smith of the *SF Weekly* reported, Wiley's sales force at corporate headquarters in New Jersey began to get nervous about the Wal-Mart chapter in LeRoy's book. Fearing a loss of sales, with the loss of the Wal-Mart account (and, likely, fear of retribution from the company in the form of not stocking other Wiley titles), headquarters began pressuring Vondeling to rescind the offer she had made to LeRoy. She refused. The pressure intensified, until Vondeling finally quit rather than back out of the deal. The contract was voided, and LeRoy was without a publisher.

What's most disturbing about the Jossey-Bass fiasco is not that Wal-Mart had a hand in it; what's disturbing is that Wal-Mart did *not* have a hand in it. Several senior sources within the imprint confirmed to Matt Smith that the move to kill the book was rooted in the fear of jeopardizing the publisher's relationship with Wal-Mart. One editor described it as "an act of self-censorship."*[3]

"Nobody begins his workweek saying, 'Gee, I've always wanted to cower before corporate behemoths, induce the resignation of a beloved senior employee, demoralize my staff, and tarnish my company's reputation in the community through censorship!'" Smith writes. With tongue firmly planted in cheek, Smith suggests Wiley publish a book titled *Censorship for Dummies*; if used correctly, he says, it could "help you do your part to strengthen the grip of giant corporations on our culture, without requiring those same corporations to muddy their hands in the process."[4]

WWBI: WILL WAL-MART BUY IT?

But sometimes hands do get muddied. In 2004, Wal-Mart canceled its orders for *America: The Book,* by Jon Stewart and the writers of *The*

---

*LeRoy's book (along with its editor) was picked up by another San Francisco publisher, Berrett-Koehler. *The Great American Jobs Scam* was scheduled for release in mid-2005.

Daily Show, published by Warner Books. The satirical best-seller contains a spread that shows the heads of Supreme Court justices pasted onto naked bodies. That same year, while *America* didn't even make it onto Wal-Mart shelves, Walmart.com finally ceased selling *The Protocols of the Learned Elders of Zion,* the bible of global anti-Semitism. Concocted by the goon squads of Russian czar Nicholas II, this malicious forgery was long passed off as the authentic work of Jewish high priests. Popular with Nazis and their latter-day disciples, like Hamas, the book claims to detail how Jews ritually chug down the blood of Christian toddlers as part of their bid for worldwide domination. While it has been widely discredited as a total fraud and condemned as racist propaganda, until September of 2004, Wal-Mart's website offered this description: "If . . . the *Protocols* are genuine (which can never be proven conclusively), it might cause some of us to keep a wary eye on world affairs. We neither support nor deny its message. We simply make it available. . . ." A host of Jewish organizations protested, but until the Anti-Defamation League complained, the book remained available. After it was removed from the website, Wal-Mart characterized the move as "a business decision."[5]

As for *America,* coauthor and *Daily Show* producer Ben Karlin admits surprise at Wal-Mart's decision to cancel its orders. "We wanted *America: The Book* to reach America, and we thought the flag on the cover would do it for Wal-Mart since they're fond of selling things with flags on them."[6]

Despite the abundance of entertainment category-killers like Barnes & Noble, Borders, Blockbuster, and Best Buy, Wal-Mart remains the leading distributor of cultural produce. It sells more DVDs, books, magazines, and CDs than any other outlet. Dreamworks executive Jeffrey Katzenberg makes regular pilgrimages to Bentonville to work out promotional deals for his latest animated excuse for a toy line.* Time Warner's *All You* magazine is one of two periodicals launched exclusively in Wal-Mart stores. Meanwhile, in the music industry, the question "Will Wal-Mart buy it?" now factors into decisions by industry executives about which artists get signed.

Wal-Mart has managed to become a battle station unto itself in our endless culture war. Under the banner of responding to customer concerns and ensuring a family-friendly environment, Wal-Mart has become a cultural gatekeeper more powerful than the Chicken Littles of the Christian Right.

Even scrubbed free of expletives, the real Slim Shady cannot stand up in its music aisles. When Sheryl Crow took a lyrical dig at the company for selling guns, her album was yanked faster than she could scream Lance Armstrong. (She lost 10 percent of her album's potential sales as a result.[7]) The flesh-filled pages of *Maxim, FHM,* and *Stuff,* the so-called lad magazines, are no longer sold on its racks.** *Cosmopolitan, Marie Claire,* and other profiteers of female image anxiety are fitted in trays sure to conceal sexually explicit taglines. Looking for the morning-after pill Preven? Hit the road, hussy. Wal-Mart's pharmacists are nobody's zygote butchers! Even Barbie's pregnant (and married) pal Midge was too hot for the toy aisle.

And yet, in less sensitive locales Wal-Mart proves more opportunistic than ideological. In Europe, for instance, it doesn't ban music or magazines. And the books deemed unfit for shelf space are available twenty-four hours a day at Walmart.com. Not unlike the

---

*As a gesture of goodwill, or perhaps as an unofficial quid pro quo, Katzenberg was one of several California-based Wal-Mart suppliers to lobby Governor Gray Davis to oppose an anti–big box bill that would've impeded Supercenters throughout the state. Davis vetoed the bill in 2002.

**While Wal-Mart is safe from the oiled-down girls of *Maxim,* one can still find plenty of flesh on the magazine rack, particularly among the automotive titles.

Republican Party, Wal-Mart nods to a culturally conservative "base," while serving a master that suffers no moral quandaries beyond profit yields.

Even the old liberal institutions are not safe—or too proud to beg. In 2003, National Public Radio gained a new sugar daddy: Wal-Mart. The company now underwrites portions of NPR's programming. It's a curious union, given that the two institutions don't snuggle up to the same audience. Tarred by conservatives as a chief tentacle of the Liberal Media, NPR caters to educated professionals who tend to shop at Wal-Mart less than the general public.[8] Neither Wal-Mart nor NPR will disclose the amount of the underwriting grant.* (In addition to funding NPR programming, Wal-Mart cut checks for the Tavis Smiley shows on both PBS and NPR, and donated $500,000 to a scholarship program for minority journalists.)

COSMO GETS A BURKA

A guy in a Florida Wal-Mart checkout line picks up a *Cosmo* from the magazine rack, for reasons that remain unclear, and becomes incensed by a headline he reads on the cover, a clever play on words that has to do with how to give a great blowjob. Furious, the man, Arthur Ally, brings the magazine to the store manager and demands that she read the article on hummers. Out loud. To him. She wisely

---

*Responding to listeners' complaints that the company is attempting to muscle NPR's editorial content, the network responded with a statement ensuring that listeners would "hear the same careful, accurate reporting on the companies and individuals who support us as you would on any other topic." NPR's ombudsman, Jeffrey Dworkin, said, however, that "NPR's protestations that the underwriting changes nothing essential sound a little nervous to me." (www.reclaimthemedia.org/print.php?story=04/02/26/4572920)

declines and advises Ally to put his complaint in writing. Ally, the founding manager of the Timothy Fund, takes her advice.

The Timothy Fund is modeled after green organizations that use mutual-fund ownership as a means to change naughty corporate behavior. Using a group of eight funds, with more than 15,000 investors, the fund outsources its stock picks to money-management firms, which it directs to steer clear of several hundred companies it identifies as "morally irresponsible." These include Wal-Mart supplier Procter & Gamble (offers domestic-partner benefits to gay employees), Johnson & Johnson (manufactures the morning-after pill Preven), and media giant Viacom (sins too numerous to name).

Banning or even concealing top-selling checkout-line staples like *Cosmo* and *Maxim* is not a decision Wal-Mart makes on a whim—or enthusiastically. Leading up to its decision to banish the lad mags, for example, Wal-Mart had been under sustained pressure from a coalition of "morally responsible" Christian investors and a collection of right-wing activist groups, usually with the words "family" or "decency" in their names.

After corresponding for several months, Wal-Mart told Ally that it had decided against changing its policies on the women's magazines.[9] In response, Ally dumped the funds' 10,000 shares of Wal-Mart stock. In the overall scheme of things, it was largely symbolic, as 10,000 shares was a drop in the cistern as far as Wal-Mart 's stock rating was concerned. Ally knew as much, so he announced the sale with a national press release that explained the reason behind his decision. Leading conservative advocacy groups like Morality in Media, the American Decency Association, and Concerned Women for America (fronted by Beverly LaHaye, wife of Left Behind series author Dr. Timothy LaHaye) rushed to Ally's side. With the help of these groups, Ally coordinated a letter-writing campaign against Wal-Mart. But instead of praying for the letters to arrive in Bentonville in impressive numbers over the course of a few months, Ally amassed a bulk of them and posted them all at once, so they would arrive at the home office with *A Miracle on 34th Street*–style impact.

Ally claims he heard nothing from the company until it publicly announced its divestiture decision in May 2003. However, he believes he had internal support from Christian fellow travelers within the company. As he later told *Forbes* magazine, during his discussions with Wal-Mart, an executive assistant identified herself to him as a Christian who supported his efforts. What's more, Randall Sharp of the American Family Association, who discussed similar moves with Bentonville years earlier, boasts of praying regularly with a senior Wal-Mart executive over the phone.[10]

Another man who does a lot of praying (though to what God one can't be sure) is Jimmy Swaggart. Back in the day when he was a titan of professional Christianity, his Louisiana-based ministry was bringing in $147 million a year from a national TV audience that stretched across oceans. In 1986, he revved things up by likening rock-and-roll to pornography. Despite his having performed with his cousin Jerry Lee Lewis, Swaggart claimed the music had since degenerated.

"It's fostering adultery, alcoholism, drug abuse, necrophilia, bestiality and you name it. It could hardly be much worse."[11] He even went so far as singling out magazines, like *Hit Parade,* that published articles about "sexually perverted" rock bands, noting that the magazines were readily available to children at stores like Kmart and Wal-Mart.

Ten days after Swaggart's comments were broadcast in the South, Wal-Mart announced it would be pulling thirty-two rock publications from its shelves. Some of the targeted titles were national publications with journalistic bona fides like *Rolling Stone*. Others, like *Tiger Beat, Super Teen,* and *Right On!* were the sort of innocuous pinup fluff devoted more to boy matinee idols than to the lords of death metal.

A few months prior to the magazine yank, Wal-Mart had also banned comedy albums by Eddie Murphy, Richard Pryor, Cheech and Chong, and Redd Foxx, and music albums by Mötley Crüe, AC-DC, Judas Priest, Wasp, and Black Sabbath.[12] Wal-Mart claimed that its decision and Swaggart's remarks were nothing more or less than a coincidence, and that its decision was based solely on "merchandising" concerns. While it pointed to an internal memo regarding these concerns that predated the preacher's broadcast by a week and a half, the company also confirmed it had spoken with Swaggart prior to the magazine yank.[13]

Over the years, Wal-Mart slowly replenished its stock of music titles, as preachers like Swaggart and other professional moralists imploded from scandals and infighting. (Swaggart liquidated his moral capital in 1988 when a rival preacher caught him with a prostitute in a New Orleans motel. "I have sinned against you all," he would later weep to his television audience before being banned by the Assemblies of God.)

With the decline of the televangelist and the subsequent rise of the Christian Coalition, the far right shifted its outrage from rock music to gays and feminists. With the exception of the occasional *Rolling Stone* issue getting tossed for a particularly racy cover, Wal-Mart has since left most periodicals of rock alone. Not so with the music.

CULTURAL GATEKEEPING

Bentonville has always refused to stock albums bearing parental-advisory stickers; but in many cases it has extended the lockdown further, for reasons less than explicit. In the 1990s, albums ranging from Nirvana's *In Utero* to the *The Beavis and Butthead Experience* were absent from Wal-Mart shelves, even though their lyrics contained no profanity. In the case of *In Utero,* Wal-Mart said it wasn't comfortable with the album's cover art: it contained embryonic imagery. But even after Geffen Records offered to hide the offensive visuals under stickers, Wal-Mart still wouldn't buy. On Nirvana's next album, the name of one track, "Rape Me," was changed to "Waif Me" which, if nonsensical, was at least Wal-Mart friendly.

Even heartland sensation John Mellencamp faced the Bentonville boot until he agreed to remove the likenesses of Jesus and Satan from the cover of his 1996 album *Mr. Happy Go Lucky.*

CULTURE WARS ON EVERY AISLE

After dropping off film for one-hour processing in a nearby Supercenter, Tami Dragone found herself being questioned by two police officers and several Wal-Mart managers. At issue were shots of her three-year-old daughter: one pictured her without her top horsing around with her father in a swimming pool; another featured her bare butt on the living room floor. They were completely innocent photos, but Wal-Mart wasn't taking any chances. Dragone later sued the company for emotional distress, but the case was dismissed.

Advice for those who actually do prefer point-and-shoot depravity to the store-bought kind (and aren't just snapping photos for your child's baby book): forget about getting your film developed at Wal-Mart. Should you submit a roll of film documenting the night you and the wife ventured into leatherland, you'll likely find your negatives returned with a tiny note reading: "We have established guidelines in our photo centers prohibiting us from printing those images which we have classified as unsuitable."

Equally unsuitable: pregnant chicks. Pregnant doll chicks. Take the case of the aforementioned Midge, friend of Barbie. In 2002, Mattel decided that, at age thirty-nine, Midge needed another child. So her doll husband, Alan, knocked her up, plastic style. Midge debuted as a radiantly pregnant mom-to-be, whose detachable, magnetic stomach came with a baby inside. While the baby was removable, Midge's wedding ring was not. Mattel marketed the toy, in part, as a vehicle for parents to talk to their children about reproduction. It was, perhaps, for this reason that Wal-Mart put the kibosh on Midge after receiving complaints from customers. According to several newspapers, the unwanted Midges were later dumped on the British market, where they proved a huge success.[14] Many in the United States and abroad couldn't help observing the irony that a store made squeamish by a pregnant doll had no reservations about selling firearms.

A KINDER, GENTLER CENSORSHIP

Standing up for a few jerk-off mags and a handful of shock-rock albums is no one's ideal First Amendment fight. But an embargo on the likes of Sheryl Crow, Eminem,* Jon Stewart, or George Carlin is far more distressing. Like it or not, they are among the most visible trumpeters of risky, against-the-grain ideas. Take Eminem, the rare cultural emissary capable of drawing fire from both sides of the culture war. Populating his aural landscape of outrage with "bitches" and "faggots," the Detroit rapper at first glance may seem nothing more than another sensationalist stunt man. But even his harshest critics won't dismiss him as having nothing to say. His anger, as he

---

*Eminem's *8-Mile* soundtrack is stocked at Wal-Mart. None of his other titles are.

puts it, has "no particular direction just sprays and sprays" but it speaks to millions. A good portion of those millions are white sub-urban and rural young men—often considered Eminem's core audi-ence. While Wal-Mart serves this population, indeed targets it, the company still denies it the ability to buy Eminem at its stores. It hardly seems a "merchandising" concern or a "retail decision."

In the case of *America: The Book,* Wal-Mart ousted one of the most routinely subversive political voices in the country—the writ-ers of *The Daily Show.* If that sounds hyperbolic, consider the sad truth that for millions of young people, *The Daily Show* is both satire *and* news source. The element of the book that Wal-Mart objected to—the nude bodies with the faces of the Supreme Court justices superimposed atop the shoulders—might, understandably, have been objectionable had they appeared on, or even near, the cover. But the nudes appear nearly one hundred pages into *America,* making it hard to imagine how they might shock the dentures off an aisle-wandering Wal-Mart granny.

Until 1996, Wal-Mart usually banned only those items whose language could reasonably be spun as not in keeping with a family-oriented store. Not so for Sheryl Crow's song "Love Is a Good Thing," which, had it even made it to the shelves, would certainly never have been heard on the store's radio network. The offending lyrics? "Watch out sister / Watch out brother / Watch our children as they kill each other / with a gun they bought at the Wal-Mart discount stores."

The ban on Crow's CD, along with the censorship of various magazines, books, and other recordings, sends a clear message to artists, record companies, and publishers alike: Wal-Mart will not tolerate dissenters. Like the brutal "positive reinforcement" tactics seen in *A Clockwork Orange,* this message is reinforced with every rejected product.

Exactly what books and movies are "Wal-Mart quality" is a

deeply political question. Why is a Christian apocalypse fantasy brimming with mass carnage and anti-Semitism more acceptable (or, as Lee Scott puts it, "inspirational") than a faked photograph of naked judges? It's hard to say, since Bentonville cloaks its decisions in the threadbare shroud of customer demand. Bentonville dismisses community opposition to its stores as the work of a "vocal minority." Could there be another vocal minority behind its merchandising decisions? How many complaints does it take to get a book off the shelves? It's like asking how many licks it takes to get to the center of a Tootsie Pop. We may never know. But the absence of explanations more substantive than "Customers were concerned" leaves one wondering who is pulling the strings. Executives and Wal-flacks continue to toe the line of one of Mr. Sam's founding principles: "respect for the individual." Why that same respect doesn't extend to an individual's right to choose which book, magazine, or movie she'd like to buy remains a mystery.

So tally it up: No emergency birth control or pregnant dolls. No lewd rap lyrics, nude photos, or album art featuring embryos or Jesus *avec* Satan. No lyrics critiquing gun policy. No spoofs on organized religion. No lad magazines about models, sex, and gadgetry.

But: Yes to guns and ammo, yes to extremist Christian novelists, and yes to . . . Paris Hilton? Michael Moore? Quentin Tarantino?

Just when you're convinced Wal-Mart is the lapdog of religious ideologues, that its colossal distribution centers will become battle fortresses in the coming culture wars, just when you're ready to up and declare a secular humanist jihad, Wal-mart does something completely unexpected.

A GAY AGENDA?

In 2001, several members of the Seattle-based civil rights group Pride Foundation journeyed to Bentonville to meet with senior Wal-Mart executives and discuss issues ranging from domestic-partner health insurance to the protection of gays and lesbians under the company's antidiscrimination policy. The Pride members requested the meeting as shareholders, not activists. Like the conservative Timothy Fund, the Equality Project, which the Pride Foundation takes part in, had purchased company stock in hopes of pressuring Wal-Mart into changing its policies on gay issues.

But unlike the Timothy Fund's boycott, the Pride Foundation's efforts didn't seem to be making a dent. Less than a year after the dialogue began, Wal-Mart's Human Resources director, Coleman Peterson, told the group in a conference call that while he appreciated the education, the company was going to handle the issue through management training. Dialogue continued through the following year, but Wal-Mart gave no indication it intended to change its policy, which did not offer specific protection for gay employees.

Then, out of the blue, Wal-Mart sent a letter to the Foundation indicating that gays, lesbians, and transgendered people were now among the groups protected under its antidiscrimination policy. Members of the Pride Foundation were left scratching their heads. Perhaps it was strictly a PR move, coming at a time when the company was reeling from criticism about its gender class-action lawsuit. Wal-Mart, however, informed the *New York Times* that it had received a letter signed by several gay employees that the current policy left them feeling "excluded." This is not the only example of an apparent fissure in Wal-Mart's ideological woodwork. *Maxim* and *Stuff* are

off the rack; in their places are any number of steamy romance novels and automobile magazines where waxed-down cars are draped
with waxed-down models.

In the run-up to the 2004 presidential elections there was much
talk about which retailers would refuse to carry Michael Moore's
Fahrenheit 9/11, timed to go on sale less than a month before the voting. CBS News declined to advertise the movie during its broadcasts
and several retailers opted to carry the film without advertising it.[15]
It might have seemed a no-brainer that Wal-Mart, which sent plenty
of political dollars Bush's way (in 2003, Wal-Mart made 85 percent
of its political contributions to the Republican Party[16]), would close
ranks around the president. After all, John Kerry (and his wife) dissed
the company on the campaign trail. Moore, too, took Wal-Mart to task
in *Bowling for Columbine,* purchasing bullets at a Canadian Wal-Mart as
a stunt. But, lo and behold, Wal-Mart peddled Moore's anti-Bush film
by the crateload.

While some Wal-Mart opponents claim the world's largest
retailer is using its clout to impose its own social agenda upon
America and the world, it's more accurate to see the company as an
accommodationist, "playing to the base," the same as any canny
politician. If Wal-Mart is so deeply committed to putting the clamp
on "offensive" books, music, and magazines, why does it check most
of these policies at the U.S. border? In the United Kingdom, Germany,
and South America, Wal-Mart doesn't play the same games with
magazines, music, or books as it does stateside. Even labor unions,
the cockroach that will never die despite Wal-Mart's best efforts,
have been accommodated in other countries. After sustained pressure
from China's state-run (and hopelessly ineffectual) labor union, Wal-
Mart agreed to stay neutral if its workers sought representation. In
Germany, the company has dealt with unions for years. And even in
the United States, where it maintains a permanent staff of union

busters, Wal-Mart will acquiesce to union construction firms if it's the only way to get a key store built.[17]

So perhaps the better question is not "Is Wal-Mart a censor?" but rather "Are Wal-Mart's conservative tendencies shaping the larger culture in its own image?"

People in cities or even populous towns might shrug their shoulders and think Wal-Mart is really just one store among many. But if your income dictates your shopping destination, what then? Everyone has some version of the story in which they stumble upon a book, an album, or some other piece of cultural detritus that forever changes their lives. The Wal-Martization of our culture helps skew this experience toward market-friendly products that a corporation (perhaps influenced by a "vocal minority") doesn't find objectionable. Does this mean every artist banned from Wal-Mart has offered the world a searing and profound critique of the human condition? Or that everyone who reads a book at age ten will never stray from its ideas? Obviously not. But it's disturbing to observe that as our stores grow in size and power, our choices grow fewer and fewer.

NINE

TAMING THE BEAST

T hey destroy local newspapers. They destroy other local businesses. They destroy individual initiative and [the] ambition
of the young people. They lead to greater concentration of
wealth in the hands of the few. They cause business dictators which
will bring Fascism to America."[1]

This passage was not culled from any fundamentalist tract or
incendiary socialist pamphlet. It does not describe a recent business
fad or the latest cultural export of savage secular humanists. Rather,
the passage is lifted from the introduction to a federal anti-chain-
store bill brought before Congress in 1938 by Representative Wright
Patman, a New Deal Democrat from Texas.

If Patman's rhetoric were dusted off and repeated on the floor of

Congress today, it would be nothing more than a one-way express ticket to the political fringe. "Business dictators" and "Fascism" in the same speech? It's enough to make Ralph Nader look like a squeaky centrist.

Yet the rhetoric is only part of the anachronism. The idea that legislation—a single bill—capable of flattening a Wal-Mart–esque company could even make it out of committee is as unlikely as the fact that its proponent was a Democrat from the capital of Planet Red State.

To understand the shift in America's reception to discount chain stores, it's necessary to revisit the early twentieth century, a time when they were an emerging concept on the American landscape.

A&P: A KINDER, GENTLER BEHEMOTH

One out of every seven cups of coffee. One of every twenty-eight eggs; one of every fourteen pounds of butter, and ten cents of every dollar spent on food in America was collected by a single corporation. It grew so fast that its patrician owner would recall that "hobos hopping off the trains got hired as managers."[2] During the height of its expansion it averaged three new stores every business day. *Time* magazine described it as a community melting pot, "patronized by the boss's wife and the baker's daughter, the priest and the policeman."

The Great Atlantic & Pacific Tea Company (A&P) was the Wal-Mart of its day, flourishing from the teens through 1950. By the latter date it had become the largest retailer in the world, bested only by General Motors as the nation's largest corporation. Though it has since retracted into a regional shadow of its former self, its business model and Wal-Mart's are kissing cousins.

Founded in 1859 by a former Maine farm boy, George H. Hartford, and New York financier George Gilman, A&P made its name distributing teas and spices in New York City and the surrounding suburbs and towns. After its cofounder sold out to Hartford, the company became a family enterprise, with the Hartford family retaining 90 percent of the stock for two generations.

It was not until the second generation of Hartfords began running things that the company became a national wonder. The idea that catapulted it was the brainchild of the middle son, John A. Hartford, Jr. He called his new concept "the economy store," and opened the first one near the company headquarters in Jersey City, New Jersey, in 1912.

It was a vision of skeletal infrastructure. All the established protocols, such as home delivery, phone orders, customer credit, and advertising were thrown to the wind. All that was needed was a lone manager, a counter, a cash register, and $1,000 worth of stock. To save on overhead, the stores were located on side streets with leases spanning no more than a year. All stores adhered to a cookie-cutter layout.

"I could walk blindfolded into any store and lay my hands on the pork and beans," Hartford would later recall. A manager could not hire so much as a part-time clerk until a predetermined sales volume had been reached.

Where Wal-Mart now boasts "Always Low Prices," A&P proclaimed it was "Where Economy Rules." And it did. As Sam Walton would later learn via Harry Weiner's panties, the gamble of drastically lowering prices while increasing volume paid off, big time.

The profit margins in A&P's economy stores were 10 to 12 percent, as compared with 20 to 22 percent at the traditional A&Ps. This recipe proved explosive, as the country experienced waves of immigration coupled with inflation in the price of food. In the first four years, the economy stores propelled A&P's total sales from $32 million to $76 million.[3]

The stores proved so successful that A&P began taking market share from competitors, and caused even more of a fuss by using its buying power to bypass wholesalers altogether. The first test came in 1915 with Cream of Wheat, the cornflakes of its day. The makers of Cream of Wheat required wholesalers and retailers to adhere to the same scale of prices. The former could buy it for 11 cents a box, then sell it to stores for 12.5 cents, with a final markup to 14 cents. Because of its size, A&P wrested the privilege to be treated like a wholesaler. But instead of charging 14 cents per unit, like everyone else, it was content to mark up only by a penny. When it refused to raise its prices, Cream of Wheat cut off shipment. A&P countered with a lawsuit, but the court ruled against it on the grounds that manufacturers had the right to set their own prices.

This prompted the company to start manufacturing its own line of products under the A&P brand. It set up its own bakeries, procured coffee direct from South American growers, and established a separate company to supply its stores with produce. At cut-rate prices, many A&P-brand products would soon outsell national brands.

Fourteen years after launching the economy store, A&P enjoyed a national market share of 7 percent, while boasting a 25-percent share in every market in which it did business. Just as Wal-Mart continues to grow during recessions, A&P came out of the Great Depression stronger than ever, hard times having made its low-price appeal ever more essential. Between 1929 and 1932, the bleakest of the Depression years, the five Hartford children earned $5 million each in dividends.[4]

A remarkable distinction between A&P and Wal-Mart, however, is in their respective attitudes toward their employees. As John A. Hartford once remarked, "The Company's responsibility to a dedicated employee is equal to that employee's responsibility to the company." It's a far cry from Wal-Mart's insistence that because its workforce is made up largely of retirees, students, and second-income earners, it's reasonable that they get their benefits through other means (read: the state).

A&P paid above industry scale and offered life and health insurance for employees long before the labor movement made such things standard. And it did not fiercely resist union organizers. As John A. Hartford told *Time* magazine, "I'm a union man myself at heart. Whatever labor got it had to get with a gun."[5] When faced with allegations of unpaid overtime, A&P set up time clocks long before that, too, became an established practice. In 1946, John and George Hartford decided to give a company-wide bonus to all 110,000 employees, each of whom received $25 in cash. The total payout amounted to 10 percent of the company's net profit for that year.

Though it enjoyed 80 percent of the national grocery market, A&P was never quite as big as Wal-Mart, even though it had 15,000 stores at its height in 1929. But A&P remained exclusively in the grocery business, where Wal-Mart has stuck its mitts into nearly every conceivable product category. Behemoths are rarely benevolent, but by the standards of today's retail environment, A&P seems to have been little more than a pussycat—a pussycat that birthed a rabid tiger.

CONGRESS VS. A&P

If set down on a carefully "quaintified" Vermont main street today, the "chains" of the 1920s and 1930s would fit seamlessly into the carefully cultivated aesthetic of nostalgia so popular in well-heeled hamlets. In the early decades of the twentieth century, these stores sprouted up like carnival tents, requiring minimal infrastructure, and often staffed by a single employee. Like Wal-Mart today, their sales figures served as proof of their popularity, especially during the Great Depression.

While the public liked the low prices chains offered, the stores were not considered a panacea for the austere economic times. Today's notion that "the consumer" is a political entity whose welfare should trump that of producers, workers, or communities had not yet crystalized. In many states, especially in the South, the appearance of chain stores was seen by some as a direct attack on the small towns. Opposition had begun to coalesce during the rise of the mail-order catalogue retailers, such as Sears, Roebuck and Montgomery Ward. As Wal-Mart would do nearly a half-century later, these mail-order companies targeted an underserved rural market. Many local newspapers refused to run their advertisements, and the stigma of ordering from a catalogue was so great that, like a purveyor of adult goodies, Sears, Roebuck began mailing its catalogues in plain brown envelopes, with the written promise of total discretion.[6] To cap it off, in the South merchants began spreading rumors that Sears, Roebuck was a black-owned company.

The A&P, whose name now functions mainly as a handle to describe the most backward of outfits, was virtually Depression-proof in the thirties. Struggling families flocked to the stores to take advantage of their low prices. Small-business owners who saw customers passing their stores up in favor of the A&P joined forces with farmers and labor unions and fought back by pushing for punitive taxes.

Walking into this political fight was Wright Patman, whose bill was a protectionist measure designed to level the playing field so the little guys could still play. Defining a chain as any company with more than ten stores, the bill proposed a graduated tax, starting at $50 per store, and capped at $1,000 for chains with more than 500 outlets. This sum was then multiplied by the number of states in which a chain did business. With 12,000 stores in forty states, A&P would have been handed a total bill of $471 million, or 30 percent of its annual sales.

Many in Congress were uncomfortable with legislation aimed, in effect if not in theory, at taking down a few specific companies. Farmer associations dependent on produce sales to the chains spoke out against the bill, as did a few emerging consumer advocates, who stressed the importance of the store's low prices in a time of economic austerity. Even organized labor, which had once been a fierce critic of the chains, reversed its position when A&P struck a deal with the AFL president, William Green: unionization in exchange for its support against the bill.[7]

Even so, Patman's bill got out of committee with seventy-five sponsors from thirty-seven states.[8] The anti–chain-store camp boasted prominent allies, most notably Louisiana's demagogic governor Huey Long, various radio personalities, and, for some time, organized labor.

The rhetoric of the chain-store opponents of seventy years ago mirrors the critique of Wal-Mart today. By 1939, no fewer than nineteen states had passed legislation that levied taxes on chains in proportion to their size. Comparing the chains of the 1930s to the Wal-Mart of today is not just an intellectual parlor game; it's more than just a need to note the forgotten history of American opposition to behemoth stores. Let's face it, long-expired state tax law and some chest-thumping rhetoric is hardly the most inspiring legacy of social protest. But that the issue was raised directly in the legislative branch of the federal government should be a stark reminder of how much has changed, while simultaneously serving as a source of inspiration as to what is possible.

Back in the thirties, the debate over chain stores was framed around one big specific question: Was A&P, and were stores of its kind, good for America? As Patman pleaded before Congress: "Will the country's interest be promoted in a better way by the million and a half retail stores being owned by more than a million local citizens, or will the country be better off if these million and a half retail stores are owned and controlled by a few childless brothers?"[9] (The "childless brothers" in question here were John and George Hartford, heirs to and owners of the Great Atlantic & Pacific Tea Company.)

To Patman and his allies, a business model that leveraged unprecedented buying power and the economy of scale to undersell competitors was an institution fundamentally at odds with American ideals of equal opportunity, even if the institution treated its employees well. After all, how many merchants in the destitute thirties could have leapt into the ring with a colossus like A&P? Was the presence of A&P—in the form it was taking—a hindrance to capitalistic fair play?

It's not that these questions aren't asked in the age of Wal-Mart, they're just asked less directly, and, perhaps more important, they are asked by those with far less political capital and with much fainter voices. Even when a magazine floats such a ponderous headline as IS WAL-MART TOO POWERFUL? the silence is deafening. The consensus is: If it is, so what?

A city councilman in Los Angeles won't come out and say he's against Wal-Mart, even as he backs an ordinance to prohibit the presence of stores measuring over 100,000 square feet. The councilman, Eric Garcetti, will instead say, "We're not saying to Wal-Mart that we don't want you under any condition. But we want to bring them to Los Angeles in a way that supplements the economic development policies we have."[10]

The rhetoric may seem timid, but today's Wal-Mart opponents engage in a resistance that's more populist, more entangled in grass roots, and more efficacious than anything witnessed by those beefing with A&P. And yet, if there's such a thing as an "anti—Wal-Mart movement," it exists primarily in the imagination of right-wing opinion writers. Whether the multifarious but modest forces uniting against the company comprise a social movement might make for an interesting master's thesis, but it is likely quite irrelevant to the actual movers. Perhaps the most fitting analogy is to the so-called antiglobalization movement, which also united a consortium of divergent factions.

But Wal-Mart resisters don't require any sort of Seattle to prove their strength. They do it all the time, tossing politics to the wind, rolling up their sleeves and smacking the grin from Rollback Smiley's insipid face. Like so many other brawls, the majority of Wal-Mart fights begin small, and they begin at home.

SITE FIGHT NATION

Out for a mid-morning walk, a middle-aged woman spies a back-hoe busy breaking ground on the once fallow lot adjacent to her subdivision. When asked, a hardhat casually tells her that a 203,000-square-foot Wal-Mart Supercenter is on its way. It will feature a gas station, a tire-and-lube express, and will be open 24/7. It will employ between 400 and 500 workers, and have parking for 1,000 cars.

Within a week, "Citizens for Wal-Mart Anywhere Else" has a webmaster, a spokesperson, and three press releases. Neighbors who knew one another only by their cars or their dogs now convene at one another's homes to brainstorm. Volunteers deliver fliers to every mailbox in the neighborhood, while others swarm grocery-store parking lots collecting signatures for petitions. Local engineers, attorneys, and media wonks offer their services gratis. Bentonville is discussed with the same hushed reverence with which hobbits speak of Mordor.

Such is the opening scene of a "site fight." While some site fighters form alliances with local unions, environmental groups, and anti-sprawl activists, the majority are decidedly local brews, and as such the makeup of these committees is often a political grab bag: homeowners freaked out about what a twenty-four-hour Supercenter will do to the resale value of their homes find themselves breaking bread with activists whose unwavering wardrobe reflects an equally unwavering conviction. Other people pop out of the woodwork because they're concerned about all the traffic the store will bring to the neighborhood, or they just don't like what they've heard about the company.

Site fights are occurring with increasing regularity in the communities where Wal-Mart chooses to build. A perpetual pain in Bentonville's ass, these dogfights take place in conservative southern exurbs, small midwestern towns, and the country's largest cities. Yet there's no formula for how they work, or if they work at all. Some drag on for the better part of a decade while others are wrapped up in a few months. In the same way the World Series might hinge on a single, late-inning pitch, a site fight can come down to a byte of arcane data buried in a traffic study or the testimony of a hydrologist.

In 2003, Bentonville admitted that between fifteen and twenty of its proposed stores for that year were scrapped due to local opposition.[11] That might not seem like much, considering it opened up 230 stores in the same year. But if the numbers included all the disputed projects being appealed by company attorneys or ones lingering in the gulag of the planning process, the figure would balloon into a number far less flattering.

Roughly half a dozen factors will determine if a town or city will mix it up with the world's largest retailer. The first has to do with whether Wal-Mart's arrival is perceived as a threat to a community's sense of self. It's a thorny, ambiguous concept, but if you've ever lived in a town or city with any sense of cohesion, you know what that communal self looks like, and whether or not Wal-Mart fits into that image.

For some communities, this image is easier to see. Older towns, with distinctive main streets, renovated homes, and well-established merchants, are often understood as oases of authenticity in a sea of gated communities and cookie-cutter condos. Oftentimes a shared historical or ethnic lineage is part of the town's culture, or there's simply pride in the quality of the schools and the general uniqueness of the town's character. In short, these are places that people understand as worth saving. But saving from whom? From what?

That a store could single-handedly subvert a town's identity perhaps cedes Wal-Mart too much power. But the deleterious effect the company has had on small businesses—a vital element of social, economic, and often political interests—has become more and more difficult to debate. And while some businesses find ways to cohabit with the giant, the fact is that some will surely close as a result.

KNUCKLEHEADS, VOCAL MINORITIES, AND OTHER CONVENIENT SCAPEGOATS

With the humility only a billionaire can muster, Sam Walton once said his company would never force itself on a community that did not want it. If ever actions belied rhetoric, then this pithy nugget of country wisdom now ranks up there with another famous Wal-Mart canard, "We're not antiunion, we're pro-associate." However, unlike so many of the chairman's sayings, this one is rarely repeated by Walton's latter-day disciples. And there's a good reason for that.

No matter how many petitions are signed, letters posted, or e-mails sent; regardless of the crowds that force city council meetings out of chambers and into high school gymnasiums; regardless of almost any show of community resistance to its presence, Wal-Mart does not back down in the face of public opposition. Like any imperial army, Wal-Mart retreats only when forced.

In the same way that it outsources responsibility for its labor malfeasance to rogue managers and other "knuckleheads," Wal-Mart dismisses local opposition as a minority phenomenon. Channeling the ghost of another straight shooter, Wal-Mart claims solid support from a "silent majority."[12] Never mind those rambunctious shows of civic participation, the thousands of signatures on petitions gathered in front of the local grocery store, roving informational pickets— none of it reflects what people *really* think. The resistance, as Wal-Mart sees it, is merely the work of an organized and outspoken cabal.

It may strike the impartial observer that a company so obsessed with data that it can determine that an approaching hurricane requires the stocking of extra strawberry Pop-Tarts has yet to conduct a single poll measuring the sound of silence. It has, on the other hand, shown a willingness to engage in a host of tactics to manipulate public opinion. Nowhere is this more apparent than in the final domestic frontier, site fighting's heavyweight arena—urban America.

FROM THE STICKS TO THE CITY

The Ozarks of northwest Arkansas gave Sam Walton a perfect laboratory. Away from the prying eyes of competitors and the media, he was able to hone his company's infrastructure, its merchandising and its distribution operations, in a somewhat more forgiving environment than a major metropolitan market. But embedded in Wal-Mart's business model, of course, is the imperative of perpetual growth.

As Wal-Mart became a national player, and particularly, as the Supercenter proved enormously successful, the company began creeping from larger suburbs and entering midsized metro areas like Tulsa and Oklahoma City. But this only brings Wal-Mart so far. Seventy percent of the food retailing business comes out of the country's top one hundred markets. In the fall of 2004, Wal-Mart was a presence in only thirty of these markets. While its International Division continues to pursue growth in foreign markets, particularly in China, the domestic agenda is being carved in city stone.

"City people don't get Wal-Mart," then executive vice president Tom Coughlin told shareholders at Wal-Mart's 2004 meeting.[13] "Wal-Mart is for country people." To what extent Wal-Mart understands city people, though, remains to be seen. Judging from its first attempts, it can be quite adept at finding a way in—but never without kicking up a shitstorm of public protest.

Few would contest Walton's argument that small-town businesses were fading before Wal-Mart opened its doors, but Wal-Mart wasn't being picked on by the media and communities merely because of its success. The charge that it kills smalls businesses without regard for a community's desires or aesthetics began surfacing before the company earned even one of its "world's largest" titles or debuted its hulking Supercenters.

The reason Wal-Mart was held accountable for gutting small towns was simple: no comparable national retailer was targeting small rural towns with the same systematic tenacity. Topping it all off was the fact that its effects on a local business community could be traced empirically.

University of Iowa economics professor Kenneth Stone has been doing that for nearly two decades. Though his first study prompted hostile phone calls from Don Shinkle and scowls from Wal-Mart store managers, Stone has maintained he bears no grudge against the company. In fact, he says he shops there regularly.

As Stone sees it, the opening of a Wal-Mart amounts to "a zero-sum game." Rather than create jobs and wealth, a new store merely reshuffles what's already there. The jobs it creates replace the ones it destroys.

In 2002, an economist at the University of Missouri, Professor Emek Basker, found much the same thing after completing two re-markably wide-ranging and long-term studies, one on Wal-Mart's effects on job creation, the other on its effects on retail prices. Analyzing 1,750 U.S. counties over twenty-seven years, Basker's findings were not wholly unkind to Wal-Mart, as the data indicated the company's entrance into a new market reduced prices on everyday items by about 5 to 10 percent.

Like Stone's study, Basker's findings exploded the idea that Wal-Mart represents a meaningful source of jobs. According to Basker, a new Wal-Mart usually posts a gain to a community of one hundred jobs, a number that fades to fifty over the next five years as other retailers go out of business.[14]

These are significant findings for many reasons, not least of which is that Wal-Mart's boosters, in the media and beyond, invari-ably herald the company's arrival in their community because it means new jobs. With the larger Supercenters, the number of jobs on the table can be as high as four to five hundred.

But where do these jobs come from? It's a question that is not asked nearly enough. When a technology firm, for example, opens in a city or town, it represents a new source of wealth. It certainly won't employ every local, but chances are high that it won't put the other tech firms out of business. Not true for retail, where there's a limited market base. If Wal-Mart were required to sell itself on the promise of creating fifty jobs over five years, one wonders, would any community buy into the hype?

THE WAL-MART VOTE

Whether in a small town, a tony burb, or city hall, "to Wal-Mart or not to Wal-Mart" is one of the touchiest questions in local politics. In hundreds of municipalities, incredulous mayors and other elected officials exclaim how they've *never* seen such a turnout for a planning-board meeting. In historically sluggish elections, "the Wal-Mart vote" becomes the only issue that matters. The emotions it unleashes can make the abortion-rights issue seem blander than a bowl of butterless oatmeal.

Since the mid-eighties, communities have organized to keep Wal-Mart out of their neighborhoods for reasons ranging from the broadly political to the narrowly self-interested. Some oppose it because of the traffic it generates, while others rail against the company's reputation on labor issues. Its deleterious effect on surrounding residential property value triggers some of the fiercest resistance. Less quantifiable but just as pervasive is the broader notion that standing up to Wal-Mart is about protecting a community's character from a blitzkrieg of homogenization that's fast turning America into a cookie-cutter nation.

In these civics-level site fights, long-standing political alliances are often strained to the breaking point. Homeowners see an unneeded, unattractive chain store forcing itself into their community. The elected salivate over the possibility of easy tax revenues. And low-income communities see a source of jobs and badly needed retail amenities. In such a complex situation, it is perhaps unavoidable that racial politics come into play when well-meaning activists, often white, don't acknowledge how their anticorporate crusade might mean depriving poor people, often black and Latino, access to groceries. Naturally, such divergent interests let Wal-Mart and its allies smear the opposition as "snobs" or, worse still, racists.

While a site fight may be won or lost on the merits of a traffic study or environmental impact statement, what brings out the crowds is a broader struggle between two competing versions of American authenticity. One is of storefronts and main streets, homegrown institutions with *Cheers*-like appeal: a place where everybody knows your name. In this romanticized vision, stores and merchants enjoy historic ties to a community and aren't simply parachuted in "from corporate."

The other American retail universe is the province of the proverbial "strip." Packed with fast-food franchises, gas-station minimarts and big-box chains, these four-lane boulevards of 24/7 commerce have become our shopping ghettos. They could not exist, much less proliferate, if nobody patronized them, and therein lies their claim to authenticity: Big-box stores are cheap and simple. Parking is free and abundant. Cavernous interiors offer anonymity, low prices, and one-stop convenience. The ascendancy of the "no frills" aesthetic has made "ugly" an elitist adjective.

Wal-Mart has long ingratiated itself to an America whose ideas of itself are often far from reality. The company's TV spots and advertising circulars feature people with bad ties and big glasses, cowboy hats and overplump midsections that are disarmingly, if also distressingly, familiar. Such a celebration of real people is refreshing; in another milieu it could be part of a social-realist experiment.

But as ubiquitous as Wal-Mart seems to be, it is strangely absent from the popular imagination. In the calendars we hang from our cubicles, the postcards we send to friends from the places we're proud to have visited, in the feel-good montages of feel-good movies, where's Wal-Mart? American iconography is still dominated by quaint small towns, colossal urban skylines, the wonders of our wilderness, and even McDonald's, Coca-Cola, and Windows' Flying Toasters screensavers. Wal-Mart and its big-box brethren are nowhere to be found.

A Cro-Magnon man joke posits the ideal woman as one who makes love until midnight and then turns into a pizza and a six-pack. It's actually not far off from our relationship with Wal-Mart: we're delighted to feed at its low-price trough, but, as is the case with garbage dumps or prisons or prostitutes, we'd just as soon not think about it until it creates a problem we can't ignore.

ADDENDUM: PYRAMID QUEST

News broke in May of 2004 that Wal-Mart was planning a 71,902-square-foot store in San Juan Teotihuacán, Mexico. Wal-Mart was already the country's number-one retailer, with more than 650 stores in sixty-six cities, so the addition of another store didn't seem like a big deal.

Except people went bat-shit.

The reason: Wal-Mart planned to build near the Pyramids of the Sun and the Moon, two-thousand-year-old remains of the Aztec empire. The protests began immediately, and with much more ire and devotion than in those anti–Wal-Mart protests seen in the United States. Hunger strikes. Pickets. Human blockades. Protesters massed at the front door of the National Institute for Anthropology and History in Mexico City—which had granted Wal-Mart a permit to build at the Teotihuacán site—making it impossible for institute employees to get to work. Political leaders claimed the company had damaged archaeological relics during the construction. Wal-Mart, for its part, stayed on message. A Wal-flack said, "Don't small towns have the right to have access to the same level of quality goods that Mexicans have in larger cities? Today, residents of Teotihuacán have to travel fifteen miles to get to the closest department store."[15]

TEN

RACE, CLASS, AND CUL-DE-SAC RADICALS: SAYING NO TO WAL-MART

THE INGLEWOOD EXPERIENCE

In 2003, eighty-two-year-old retired nurse Annie Lee Martin opened her mailbox to find, among the other pieces of ubiquitous direct mail, an oversized postcard from Wal-Mart. This wouldn't have been so unusual, had Martin's face not been emblazoned on the front of the postcard, along with words of support for an upcoming ballot measure to determine whether Wal-Mart would be allowed to open a Supercenter in Inglewood. The words attributed to her were, she claimed, words she never spoke or wrote ("I hope you will join with me in voting Yes on Measure 4A").

A few weeks earlier, as she arrived home from a trip to the grocery store, Martin told the *LA Weekly,* she had been approached by

Wal-Mart representatives, one of whom had a camera. They mentioned that they were from the company, and were trying to get a store into Inglewood. Martin says they asked her if they could take her photograph. Oblivious to the politics behind the issue, and a fan of Wal-Mart herself, Martin agreed. She even signed a paper at the request of a Wal-Mart representative, assuming it was nothing more than a petition indicating her support for the store. "I signed a blank piece of paper," Martin told the *LA Weekly*.[1]

Greater Los Angeles is home to several self-governing cities. West Hollywood and Santa Monica are two famous examples, each known for harboring the rich, the famous, and thousands of guys who were in, like, you know, the commercial for that lite beer?

A lesser-known civic entity is Inglewood, a working-class suburb twelve miles south of downtown L.A., with a population of about 113,000 and a demographic that breaks down roughly forty percent each for African-Americans and Latinos, with whites and Asians making up the balance.

In 2003, Wal-Mart announced plans for a 200,000-square-foot Supercenter on the sixty-acre former site of Inglewood's Hollywood Park racetrack. The pitch from Wal-Mart featured the usual economic lap dance of increased sales-tax revenue for the city, low prices for the consumers, and jobs, jobs, jobs. The city's main Wal-Mart proponent was its mayor, who saw the deal as "a no-brainer." The four-member city council, however, was of quite a different mind. They rejected the proposal four to none.

Inglewood was never going to be your typical site fight. Because it was to be home to the first Supercenter in metro L.A., one of forty such stores Wal-Mart had planned for the Golden State, it would be an extremely high-profile campaign. The eyes of developers, the retail industry, organized labor, and other Wal-Mart opponents were trained on the community, and the fight. The outcome, it seemed, would be an indicator of what lay in store as the company migrated into urban America.

At the ballot measure's onset, the union at the heart of many big site fights was up to its ears in the southern California supermarket strike, so the reins of the opposition were handed over to the Los Angeles Association for a New Economy (LAANE). A union-funded think tank, LAANE was known and respected in progressive circles for having pushed an ordinance requiring all city contractors to pay a living wage. LAANE was the driving force behind the Latino-oriented labor resurgence in the 1990s that made L.A. a union power base, with big organizing victories for home health aides, janitors, and hotel workers.

With Inglewood's city council denying Wal-Mart the front door, the company opted for the back: a ballot measure. Under the terms of the proposed measure, Wal-Mart could do anything shy of declaring itself an independent republic (although some thought that was exactly what Wal-Mart was up to; one writer said that it "was trying to establish a sovereign state inside the city of Inglewood"[2]). Buried in the ballot measure's fine print was a set of restrictions and caveats custom-designed to ensure Wal-Mart would not be handcuffed. For instance, the plan would have Wal-Mart, not the city, conducting its environmental and traffic reviews. Wal-Mart would be free to change the style of the store's signs, or any other aspect of the development, and the city would have no say in the matter. And even though Wal-Mart's measure needed a mere majority to pass, it could be rescinded only with the sanction of two-thirds of Inglewood's electorate.[3]

Wal-Mart began paying canvassers to collect the signatures necessary to get the ballot before the voters,* and hired a local PR firm geared toward African-Americans and Latinos. The African-American

---

*According to activists in LAANE, Wal-Mart paid the petition-gatherers more than it paid its cashiers.

media were flooded with the company's "Good Jobs First" ads, and small newspapers featured full-page ads trumpeting the store as a boon to the community.

ROLLBACK SMILEY MEETS TAVIS SMILEY

Local son and then NPR mainstay Tavis Smiley welcomed a surprise guest to his Los Angeles studios on the eve of the Inglewood vote: Lee Scott. In the interest of full disclosure, Smiley informed his radio audience that Wal-Mart was an underwriter of his show, then proceeded to lob the kind of question normally seen on *Access Hollywood* or *Entertainment Tonight*.

"I've had the chance to, as you know, come to Bentonville and to speak to the employees at Wal-Mart," Smiley said, "and . . . I was blown away by the fact that everybody calls you Lee. I mean, here you are the CEO of the company, but everybody from the receptionist to the janitor calls you Lee."[4]

When Smiley floated the charge that Wal-Mart discourages union organizing, Scott answered by extolling the company's "open-door policy," which permits associates to bring their concerns to managers without fear of retaliation. Smiley chose to forgo the obvious follow-up question—namely, to ask the CEO how such a policy could possibly be equal to the power of collective bargaining. Worse, Smiley never mentioned the ferocious battle going on in Inglewood, despite his taking the opportunity to remind his audience that he was a resident of the black community. *LA Weekly*'s Erin Aubry Kaplan observed seismic obfuscation in Smiley's journalistic performance on his PBS television interview with Scott the day before.

"He told the cameras once again that he resides in the 'hood, right across the street from the Crenshaw Wal-Mart; yet he never brought up the fierce opposition in nearby Ingle-hood to a ballot measure that by any analysis would have seriously disempowered the majority black local government," Kaplan wrote. "He ignored the fact that black leadership all over the state came out of the woodwork to oppose the measure, and the fact that they all charac-terized it as a big step backward in the ongoing fight for civil rights, economic justice and self-determination. In short, Smiley did not address the very reasons why he was compelled to do a Wal-Mart show in the first place."[5]

Scott's appearance wasn't a random visit. It was politically timed to pander to African-American Inglewood residents on the eve of the vote that would determine not only if Wal-Mart would become a part of the community, but whether it would be able to make Ingle-wood the sort of beachhead needed to push into California's most populous markets.

Jobs. Low prices. A major company showing confidence in the area. What was so bad about letting Wal-Mart in? What was all the fuss about? For many of Inglewood's residents, Wal-Mart's low prices were impossible to ignore. As in many communities, making ends meet was more pressing than making a sociopolitical statement. And yet, to many in Inglewood, that was exactly what was happening: they were being asked to make an ambiguous political statement instead of taking proper care of their bills and their families. The question for organizations like LAANE, though, was how to frame the fight, and how to organize the opposition.

In the case of Inglewood, despite its pro-union leanings, emphasiz-ing Wal-Mart's alleged labor abuses was not the way to go. Wal-Mart site fights are sometimes organized around the company's reputation on labor issues, but this tack can be a slippery slope, particularly when organized labor is bankrolling the opposition. Who cares about a scrap between two well-oiled interest groups? And hell, for that matter, when was the last time a labor union offered you a "Bratz Live in Concert Cloe" doll for $14.97?

So even though Inglewood boasted over 10,000 union households, LAANE didn't frame its campaign around labor issues. "It was about respect," says LAANE executive director Madeline Janis-Aparicio, referring to the company's perceived lack of deference to Inglewood's system of home rule. In some ways it was only a matter of letting Wal-Mart's hubris do LAANE'S work for them; the company's insistence on going over the head of local government rubbed many the wrong way, even those in the community who would've otherwise welcomed Wal-Mart with open arms.

On April 6, 2004, Inglewood voters sent Wal-Mart packing by a margin of 60 percent to 40. This no-vote prevented the company from establishing a dangerous precedent—eliminating or bypassing community control over that community's own development process. Voters, it seemed, had seen through the propaganda. Wal-Mart's strategy, one community website read, was clear: "(1) Come into town, study existing (locally-controlled) stores' prices and undercut them, even taking a loss until all local competition is eliminated. (2) Send profits back to Bentonville. . . . (3) Once hegemony is gained over the community, close its store, consolidating it into a Superstore further away."[6] Despite the company's clear loss, Wal-Mart once again claimed it was the victim of special interests.

"We are disappointed that a small group of Inglewood leaders, together with representatives of outside special interests, were able to convince a majority of Inglewood voters that they don't deserve the job opportunities and shopping choices that others in the L.A. area enjoy," Vice President for Government Affairs Bob McAdam told the *New York Times*.[7]

One doesn't have to follow the money very far to see that Wal-Mart's claims hold little water. Los Angeles's Central Labor Council, a local consortium of AFL-CIO–affiliated unions, threw $110,000 into the Inglewood fight. Wal-Mart spent nearly ten times that amount.

Five months after the defeat in Inglewood, Lee Scott confessed that perhaps Wal-Mart's strategy was not ideal.

"Had we gone to the city council and been treated fairly, I think we could have gone to the voters and seen a different result. We did not do that as well as we should have done," Scott said in a speech at the Goldman Sachs global retailing industry conference.[8] Absent from the CEO's comments was any acknowledgment that it was the substance of the ballot measure, and not only the way the company went about the business of bringing its business to the neighborhood, that ticked off Inglewood residents.

Elsewhere, Wal-Mart has co-opted not just local democracy, but has even perverted union rhetoric to speak to its own cause. In Taos, New Mexico, for example, Wal-Mart found its plans to expand an existing discount store into a Supercenter tabled when the city council approved a new zoning code. Wal-Mart's response? Beginning its own faux grassroots campaign to encourage citizens to put the question to a vote. The company used a slogan coined by that champion of big business and corporate profit making César Chávez: ¡Sí se puede!

GROCERY GAPS
AND OTHER OPPORTUNITIES

The fallen idols of American retail spent much of the past fifty years in pursuit of an affluent customer base as it migrated from city to suburb. Downtown "flagship" stores were shuttered in favor of the burgeoning shopping malls. Wal-Mart's path, though, has been the reverse commute. Established originally in rural areas ignored by larger retailers, the company's urban strategy follows a similar path by targeting neglected sectors of the urban market.

In the Crenshaw section of South Central Los Angeles; in downtown Hartford, Connecticut; in deindustrialized west Chicago; and in other struggling, often minority communities, Wal-Mart moves in where its competition won't, or even in places from which it has fled. Typically poor, and less concerned with Wal-Mart's reputation for labor malfeasance or for squeezing out small businesses, these communities are far more interested—and in need of—affordable, convenient places to shop.

The absence of the chains has created what is now a familiar phenomenon on the landscape of urban inequality. Activists call it "the grocery gap," a pervasive lack of quality, affordable food in low-income communities. Even as cities have been rebounding since their nadir in the seventies, supermarkets in the 'hood are still scarce, expensive, and poorly stocked. As recently as a few years ago, for example, the ratio of inner-city Detroit residents to chain grocery stores was more than *110,000:1.*[9]

The real insult, though, lies less in the scarcity of stores than in the inferior, often inexcusable, quality of their meat and produce, and in the prices they charge, which are often markedly higher than at the chain's stores in the suburbs. Lacking the buying power of their chain cousins, and often facing steeper insurance rates on account of their location, many ghetto marts are forced to raise prices in order to survive. Price-gouging is also a reality, since inner-city stores enjoy a semicaptive customer base of people who don't have the option of hopping in their cars for better deals down the interstate.

Wal-Mart's ability to bridge the grocery gap, even if unintentional, is arguably the biggest reason why it does not meet the level of community-based opposition in low-income neighborhoods that it does in the burbs. Unfortunately, many anti–Wal-Mart activists ignore this reality, and this failure has driven a wedge between white progressives and the minority communities they claim to advocate for. Where the former regard Wal-Mart's arrival as a clear cause for alarm (increased homogeneity, antiunion activity, overseas labor, etc.), the latter often can't help seeing it as an improvement in their lives (affordable and healthy food, convenience, and jobs—any jobs).

The bottom line is that many anti–Wal-Mart activists have incomes that allow them the luxury of cultivating a global social conscience. It's harder to care about sweatshop workers in Bangladesh when you can barely afford your baby's formula, and when it's on sale at the Wal-Mart two blocks away, well, that's where you're going to buy it.

Such was the tense situation on the east side of Nashville when a lefty activist group hosted a meeting about the arrival of a Wal-Mart Supercenter on Gallatin Road. Organizers for the Tennessee Alliance for Progress never intended to coordinate any sort of site fight, as the store was, by then, a fait accompli. Rather, the meeting was to discuss larger issues surrounding the new Wal-Mart, and its likely effects on the community. But the activists who were so concerned about Wal-Mart were not from the community.

At the meeting, the activists—mostly white, mostly middle-class—droned on about Wal-Mart's reliance on sweatshop labor abroad and its antiunion practices at home. Local residents who'd learned of the meeting that day from the daily paper were not moved. That the activists didn't directly reach out to them smacked of a snub; that none of them actually lived near the store smelled even worse. As Sam McCullough, a neighborhood-association chairman, told the *Nashville Scene*, "That's one of the most blighted areas on Gallatin Road, but they don't have to live with that because it's not in their neighborhood. Wal-Mart is the first company to show an interest in our area in 25 years."[10] An elderly woman angrily remarked to the meeting's organizers, "Whenever we black folks want something, you white folks want to take it away."[11]

As *Nashville Scene*'s Matt Pulle would later concede, "It was hard for me not to sympathize with the older black residents. You had a young white woman talking about labor conditions in Central America who admits that she buys all her groceries at an expensive organic market, while others in the room were thinking how they have to drive five miles just to buy fresh fruit."

In east Nashville, the Wal-Mart displaced a boarded-up home, a trailer park, and a used-car lot. A Supercenter set for Chicago's Austin neighborhood will go up on the site of the vacant Helene Curtis cosmetics factory. In South Central L.A., a Wal-Mart arrived in a shopping mall that had lain derelict since Macy's bailed out five years earlier. As visually unpleasant as a Supercenter might be, only the most delusional nostalgist could support the status quo of non-development.

One of the most reliable rallying cries of Wal-Mart opponents, "Save the mom-and-pops," is usually a nonstarter in poor inner-city neighborhoods. With the exception of a few beauty parlors, liquor stores, and check-cashing outfits, there are precious few mom-and-pops to save.[12]

As Wal-Mart pushes into cities, these moves serve as effective insulation against bad publicity, while breaking down historic alliances among liberals, labor, and minorities. Wal-Mart may fancy itself the savior of minority urbania, and how long this idea can remain believable is anyone's guess. But for opponents, particularly those outside the communities, to argue that Wal-Mart will wreak terror upon a community that's already terrorized is almost always a losing gambit.

WILL THE REAL ELITISTS
PLEASE STAND UP?

Hell hath no fury like a homeowner scorned. And it doesn't take The Donald to figure out that a parking lot lit up like Giants Stadium, eighteen-wheelers barreling down residential streets at all hours of the day and night, and a big, ugly box won't exactly increase the value of your home.

There's little question that Wal-Mart has a lot more to offer communities that are getting by on a lot less. So perhaps it follows that one of the most common means of smearing its opponents is by crying "elitist." Even *National Review,* an organ hardly known for its concern with economic inequality, says that "there's a lot of snobbery in hating Wal-Mart."[13]

The charge goes something like this: Incapable of grasping the fact that many Americans can't afford to shop their conscience, anti–Wal-Mart hysteria undermines the economic needs of the store's working-class base—the same people to whom so many liberals profess their allegiance.

The line of reasoning is seductive and has some truth to it. If consumerism has done anything to American political discourse, it's furthered the notion that what we buy and where we buy it serve as windows into our very souls, and the idea coalesces with our obsession with America's red-state/blue-state cultural divide: within hours of George W. Bush's reelection, the media were already crediting the GOP sweep to the "Wal-Mart Republicans."

If Wal-Mart is a red-state thing and its opponents are blue-state elitist latte liberals, then why do Wal-Mart's opponents often not fit into the left–right, latte–Dunkin' Donuts continuum? The answer, in a word, is NIMBY, or "not in my backyard," the term used to both describe and deride a knee-jerk opposition to soup kitchens, halfway houses, prisons, or mental clinics in, or even near, a residential neighborhood. The motivation behind NIMBYism may be masked by fears of increased crime rates or threats to personal safety, but it usually boils down to raw self-interest, the idea that bringing an "undesirable element" into a neighborhood will deflate the resale value of your house.

Without a doubt, NIMBYism explains some of the resistance to Wal-Mart, especially when a proposed store abuts a residential subdivision. But when developers, contractors, and others supping at Wal-Mart's expansive trough cry NIMBY, they are serving their own interests, too. Obviously, fighting off the world's largest corporation and shouting down a soup kitchen are two different endeavors with very different moral implications. Implying moral equivalency would be laughable if it were not so common. Like the rest of the Wal-Mart story, the real story—the right thing to do—is ambiguous.

WHY DO WE NEED *ANOTHER* WAL-MART?

Until the 1990s, Thornton, Colorado, was a quiet bedroom community a few exits north of downtown Denver, on Interstate 25. But throughout the decade, Californians began pouring in, and Thornton blossomed into an exurban city with a population over 100,000, independently governed but still largely dependent on Denver as its economic base.

Around Christmas 2003, word got out that a Wal-Mart Supercenter was in the works for a fifty-acre spread beside a new I-25 off-ramp at 136th Avenue. Locating on what was anticipated to be a major intersection, the site had another snag in that it bordered on the most hallowed of suburban grounds, the municipal golf course.

The store would also sit only a few miles down the interstate from another Wal-Mart Supercenter, then currently under construction.

"Why do we need another Wal-Mart?" Sue Kuhl recalls asking herself.[14] A college legal instructor, the mother of two was quick to dive into the organizing efforts, which took the form of an impromptu organization called Residents United for Thornton (RUFT).

"We had a website immediately," Kuhl said. "We hired people, we had community volunteers, we had neighborhood pickets holding signs, we had signs on the front lawn. Not only did we have a local paper cover it, we had community members with big media contacts at the *Denver Post* and the *Rocky Mountain News,* so we had reporters calling left and right."

Media saturation can be a wonderful thing, but it's not always as helpful as packing the city council chambers with warm bodies. And yet sometimes even that fails. In Thornton, the eight-member city council had to approve the proposed rezoning and, if that was approved, vote on the Wal-Mart proposal itself. The first vote, in mid-March, drew hundreds of people.

"They had to turn people away," said Jim Hardin, a former Wal-Mart employee who helped organize the opposition. "This was the first time the community got up and opposed what the city council was doing."[15] The meeting dragged on until two in the morning. Despite the opposition's attacking the specifics of the traffic study and showing strength in numbers, jaws dropped as the council approved the rezoning.

RUFT faced grim prospects as the mayor and other city councillors were quoted in the local media affirming their support for the project. Their reasons were the staple arguments of Wal-Mart boosters: more jobs, more sales taxes, and more shopping choices. RUFT responded by announcing in press conferences and through other media that it intended to turn its fight against the proposal into a referendum on their elected officials, those Wal-Mart enablers who had voted for the rezoning. RUFT began gathering signatures to recall the mayor, who, only a few months earlier, had been reelected with 80 percent of the vote. It was all they could do.

THERE'S COMMERCIAL— AND THERE'S "COMMERCIAL"

Retailing's very own answer to the other Bush doctrine, namely, that consumerism = patriotism, Wal-Mart seems to make no distinction between consumers and the neighborhoods that they call home. It can be amusing to see a corporation so often self-described as "folksy" so incapable of understanding why a 200,000-square-foot 24/7 Supercenter just doesn't wash with most Americans' idea of a neighborhood store.

"There's commercial," says John Myers, a Springfield, Illinois, lawyer, "and then there's commercial."[16] A land-use attorney and a self-professed Republican, Myers offers his services free of charge to the Southwest Springfield Neighbors Association, another community organization formed on a moment's notice to repel a proposed 205,000-square-foot Supercenter slated to occupy land within 300 feet of residential property.

The Southwest Springfield Neighbors Association came together in a hurry when district alderman Bruce Strom networked anxious constituents who had recently contacted him about the project. Rumors had been circulating even before April 2004, when the daily local newspaper reported that Wabash Avenue, on the city's southwest side, was one of two sites Wal-Mart was considering in Springfield. Four miles west of downtown Springfield, the southwest side consists of approximately a thousand homes spread out in four subdivisions. Wabash Avenue is the main thoroughfare, but it is merely a two-lane road with no divided center or left-turn lanes. While it boasts a few car dealerships and small office buildings, there's no existing big box on the strip.

A meeting was quickly arranged at the home of resident Sue Hines. With zoning requests to be heard by the city in a mere three weeks, there was no time to waste. Hines's next-door neighbor, Roger Kanerva, a retired EPA planner, recalls the group's agreeing that their arguments against the proposal were strong enough to wage a serious resistance campaign. The issues to focus on, they agreed, were roads and traffic. The development stock in West Springfield is flat former agricultural land, and it experiences problems with stormwater drainage. Wal-Mart's proposal offered no onsite drainage. Its traffic study was laughable, as it simply assumed that the nearest main artery, Wabash Avenue, would be widened to three lanes, a project presumably funded by the state. The Illinois Department of Transportation, however, had no plans for widening, and had even told Wal-Mart that Wabash Avenue would be an unacceptable outlet for store traffic. Denied access through the main roads, then, customer traffic would invariably be diverted into the lanes of the surrounding subdivisions. And considering that Springfield's largest elementary school stood near the site's eastern edge, with hordes of kids on bikes and on foot moving to and from the school, it could, arguably, prove dangerous to the community.

Wal-Mart offered some modifications. It shifted the store a few hundred feet to the south, to avoid having to ask for a rezoning permit. It also nixed its planned auto center and several "out lots" (spaces reserved as satellite businesses on the site—most often gas stations).

Yet however much it portrays itself as deeply attentive to community concerns, Wal-Mart rarely changes its plans on the basis of feedback from residents. Unless legally required, it holds no community meetings to seek input from neighbors, nor does it engage in any effort to open a dialogue with those in the community who are opposed to a store. As one Wal-flack told PBS, "We sometimes send out a postcard or hold a neighborhood meeting to identify our supporters. Opponents, they identify themselves."[17]

No neighborhood association can possibly match Wal-Mart's financial resources; still, one advantage many middle-class communities enjoy is a pool of readily available professionals with relevant skill sets. In West Springfield, for example, a retired Environmental Protection Agency regulator, a state trooper, a land-use attorney, and a computer programmer all came forward and lent their expertise to the fight. In Monument, Colorado, a six-year Supercenter scrap involved residents who served on the same county planning board they had to present their case to. Others were developers themselves, and thus more than a little familiar with traffic studies, site plans, and zoning laws.

Other times, professional credentials are less important than due diligence. In West Springfield, as in many other towns, neighbors quickly amassed petitions signed by thousands opposed to the project.

Even though development is assessed using a set of preexisting criteria, sending a clear message to elected officials that Wal-Mart is not welcome can create the suggestion of political consequence to public servants who may otherwise be inclined to see all development as a net gain.

THE MIGHTY NORTHWEST:
THE LEFT COAST VERMONT

One state that's been feeding Wal-Mart a steady diet of whup-ass is Oregon. Like many other so-called blue states, Oregon flirts with both ends of the political spectrum. Its big cities, Portland and Eugene, are liberal enclaves surrounded by conservative rural areas marked historically by agricultural production and men with guns.

In the 1970s, Oregon passed a series of land-use laws to preserve its farmland and wilderness. One feature of the legislation was the requirement that every city and county produce a master plan outlining a course for development. Many of these contain a determination of an urban-growth boundary, a line that sets a limit, in theory if not always practice, on how far new development can go. These policies have helped keep the state from seeing the same kind of haphazard sprawl seen elsewhere in the country. In such a context, Wal-Mart's push into Oregon's suburbs and small towns has met with major upsets. Between 2002 and 2004, nearly half a dozen prominent locations have flipped Rollback Smiley the bird.

In 2003, the tony Portland suburbs of Beaverton, home to Nike's headquarters, and Hillsboro thwarted a proposed Supercenter to be set across the street from a private high school. Because the location would sit at the confluence of two major roads, where traffic was already heavy during rush hours, the proposal drew the instant enmity of the Tualatin Valley Junior Academy, whose students set up roving pickets.[18] Making their case almost exclusively on the basis of traffic issues, Beaverton/Hillsboro opponents had no trouble convincing the Board of County Commissioners that the store would make an already bad traffic situation even worse. As in West Springfield, Wal-Mart's traffic study bore little relation to local volume realities, and was instead based on information from Wal-Marts in rural Oregon. Wal-Mart appealed the county's decision to Oregon's land-use board of appeals, an option not afforded in every state, and one that Wal-Mart has taken considerable advantage of. The board sided with the community. Despite such unwavering opposition,

Wal-Mart went to the Oregon Court of Appeals. The court refused to hear the case.[19] (Similar actions have been taken in Oregon City, Medford, and LaGrange.)

Sixty miles east of Portland, in the resort and sport town of Hood River, Citizens for Responsible Growth fought Wal-Mart's plans to close an existing Wal-Mart variety store and open a 185,000-square-foot Supercenter a few miles outside town. The campaign was difficult and expensive for residents, who raised and spent more than $63,000 over three years. The group hired a dream team of support that included not only a Portland attorney but also traffic, land-use, and environmental consultants intimately familiar with the specifics of the plan. Their argument? Not a word of supplier-squeezing, low wages, or gender discrimination. Instead, the group focused on why such a large store is incompatible with land situated on a flood plain, across the road from the historic Columbia Gorge Hotel.

Christine Cook is the attorney for the Hood River opponents, as well as several other Oregon towns in the same predicament. She says many of her clients' fights boil down to a battle between hydrology experts. Their hydrologists versus Wal-Mart's. Cook said her clients educate themselves and work to find areas where they can win.

Much to the delight of Cook's clients, the Hood River Board of County Commissioners rejected the Supercenter, based on its incompatibility with the area. Again, Wal-Mart appealed the county's decision to Oregon's land-use board of appeals, and was rejected.*

---

*Oregon has also made it clear to the retailer that it won't put up with labor abuses; it was in Oregon that a federal jury found Wal-Mart guilty of forcing eighty-three employees to work unpaid overtime between 1994 and 1999.

HATING WAL-MART:
A DOUBLE-EDGED SWORD

Don't like Wal-Mart's labor practices? Its increasing dependence on Chinese imports? Its power to vaporize American manufacturing jobs? Its general coziness with the Bush administration? Are you appalled by the systematic discrimination endured by associates of an inconvenient gender, or the swiftness with which the company swoops down to pick off union organizing efforts? Maybe you think its big-box stores are an aesthetic abomination?

That's cool. But when it comes to the long slog of keeping Wal-Mart out of town, it's probably best to stifle your inner Wal-Mart hater, lose the politics, and focus on the unsexy concerns of the proposal. At this point, just the name Wal-Mart can draw all kinds of people to a campaign to keep it out of your town—people who for any number of reasons don't need specifics about floodplains or tax-incremental financing schemes to know why a monster store is not right for their town.

However, when presenting a case before a city council, practical specifics are all that matter. Going the progressive, moral-outrage route is useless. Undermining Wal-Mart's traffic study by showing how it's based on irrelevant data is a far harder slap to Rollback Smiley's dumb grin than a thousand references to antiunionism or Chinese sweatshops.

Kate Huseby understands this situation better than most. A realtor in Hood River, Oregon, she devoted countless hours over three years to fighting the new Supercenter. Not surprisingly, Huseby and others in Citizens for Responsible Growth (CFRG) aren't big Wal-Mart fans. But pragmatism requires that they temper their anti–Wal-Martism, since Hood River already has a Wal-Mart. Built in the early nineties, it's the traditional variety-store kind, at 72,000 square feet. Like other longtime residents, Huseby believes Wal-Mart's presence hastened the shuttering of several downtown general stores, and she was none too thrilled by the prospects of what a supersized spawn would do to the remaining merchants. However, at this point the store is largely accepted, and CFRG claims to support its continued presence.

A similar dynamic surrounds a divisive debate in Stoughton, Wisconsin. As in Hood River, Wal-Mart aims to trade up from an older variety store to a spanking-new Supercenter located in the main growth area on the northern edge of town. Eighteen miles south of Madison, Stoughton boasts a population of 12,000 and is famous for its Norwegian heritage, which goes back nearly a century and a half. On May 16, the town hosts the largest Syttende Mai (Norwegian Constitution Day) festival this side of Oslo.

Its politics have traditionally run to the left, favoring Kerry to Bush in 2004 by 61 percent, and returning liberal senator Russ Feingold to Congress by an even higher margin. Stoughton retains some light manufacturing in the form of two plants, Uniroyal and Nestlé.

With a downtown composed of independent storefronts, it may not stand to reason that a pro–Wal-Mart, anti–smart growth organization sprouted up after the city council passed an ordinance capping all stores at 50,000 square feet. In the elections that followed, the pro–Wal-Mart group, calling itself Recapture Stoughton, seized five city council seats. One of Recapture Stoughton's most effective tactics was to spread rumors among the large senior population that if Wal-Mart didn't get its way, it would close its existing store.

"[Stoughton is] eighteen miles from Madison, so the seniors

would be especially affected if Stoughton was left without general merchandise,"[20] Kevin Pomeroy of 1000 Friends of Wisconsin said. Pomeroy believed the opposition excelled at framing any challenge to growth as being "anti–Wal-Mart." Shortly before the Supercenter debate began heating up, the state of Wisconsin approved a bill requiring municipalities to produce "smart growth" plans aimed at containing runaway sprawl. In Stoughton, the process was $80,000 underway when Recapture Stoughton used Wal-Mart, the council's approval of a big-box ordinance, and the rise of "smart growth" as a means to play divide and conquer.

Part of what helped Stoughton's pro–Wal-Mart faction gain power was a division within the leadership of the group challenging the Supercenter calling itself Uff Da Wal-Mart. (*Uff da* is Norwegian for something akin to "Oh no" or "Enough!") The group's leader, Leslie "Buzz" Davis, was a retired government planner and former city councilman with a tendency to polarize. His public statements were nakedly anti–Wal-Mart; in newspaper editorials he called the company "the piranha of American capitalism."[21]

Others in Uff Da Wal-Mart were less comfortable with the idea of turning the city-council election into a de facto Wal-Mart referendum. With the town's existing Wal-Mart open seventeen years, it was a delicate task to criticize the company without appearing to be a Wal-Mart hater. As Pomeroy explains, "People were there because they thought it was the wrong location for the store, or they didn't like being bullied by Wal-Mart."

In the end, Recapture Stoughton was able to out-organize the progressives on the city council. Critics of development were tarred as a radical ideologues, whose liberal notions were being force-fed to citizens by "fancy consultants" and Madison elites.

Within other communities, the pitfalls of excessive anti–

Wal-Martism have become obvious. "This is not an anti–Wal-Mart campaign," Roger Kanerva of the Southwest Springfield group said. "We've gone out of our way to make this clear. Making it all about Wal-Mart changes the flavor of the whole debate, [from] whether the development site is any good or not to whether or not this company is good or not."[22] A few thousand miles to the west, Jim Hardin, the former Wal-Mart associate from the store's early days in Colorado, says much the same thing.

"We didn't attack Wal-Mart per se; we attacked the people who were allowing Wal-Mart to come in. It doesn't take a rocket scientist to figure out that Wal-Mart has deep pockets. They don't really care what an individual's opinions are. If we chose to take on Wal-Mart specifically we'd lose."[23]

Instead, Hardin helped make sure it was a standing-room-only crowd at city council meetings and casually floated the word "recall" in public statements. Lo and behold, after three months of balls-to-the-wall organizing, Residents United for Thornton succeeded in forcing a 180-degree shift in their city council. Not only did they reject the store's proposal, but they enacted a big-box ordinance to ensure the issue would not resurface anytime soon.

Ninety miles south on Interstate 25, in the tiny town of Monument, John Heiser's band of retirees, young families, and a handful of high school students reached the same conclusion. However, it was a position that evolved after considerable debate over the five years the group organized.

"At one point," Heiser recalls, "I'd approached some of the union reps and talked with them. At that time they were staging protests at the Wal-Marts. One of their big things is that Wal-Mart workers make low wages. That was not really something that we could expect county commissioners to say, 'Yeah, I'll vote no on that.'"

CUL-DE-SAC RADICALS

Wal-Mart is treated to a Happy Meal of public subsidies while the rest of the kids are eating cafeteria food. According to Good Jobs First, Wal-Mart often receives from local, state, and federal government offices:

- free or reduced-price land
- infrastructure assistance
- tax-increment financing
- property tax breaks
- state corporate income tax credits
- sales tax rebates
- enterprise-zone (and other zone) status
- job-training and worker-recruitment funds
- tax-exempt bond financing

With this kind of financial and political heft on its side, it's no wonder community activists oftentimes shrink back in the face of the behemoth. But best-selling author and incurable cornpone Jim Hightower believes site fights have the potential to "unleash the latent American radicalism" in middle-class fuddy-duddies.[24] The logic goes something like this: the arrogance with which Wal-Mart imposes itself into places it's not wanted, and the rough road of resistance that ensues will miraculously turn NIMBYs into Wobblies. Such salt-of-the-earth imaginings may keep *The Nation* in print, but it gets site fights all wrong.

Let's face it, these days most forms of "unleashed American radicalism" put creationists on school boards and label state-sanctioned gay monogamy a greater social threat than having millions of people without health insurance. Wal-Mart's hometown opponents don't see themselves as terribly subversive. If anything, they see the company's aggressiveness and its flagrant disregard for their concerns as the real radical element. These are people trying to set things right so their back-porch view won't include a thousand-car parking lot and a black tar roof with satellite gear.

Pundits less reliant on populist shtick are of different minds on the site-fight phenomenon. Some write the whole thing off as an orchestration of the labor movement.[25] Others dismiss it as "pretentious snobbery," or as a collective case of irrationality that fails to understand how low prices and ensuing tax revenues trump all other concerns. While this is arguably true in some cities Wal-Mart has come to occupy, the vast majority of site fights are small-town, small-city, and exurban affairs that have nothing whatsoever to do with unions. In the larger grid of Wal-Mart resistance, site fights are important, but they're still a mixed bag. No umbrella organization exists to coordinate, or even advise, their efforts. Certainly, a lack of centralization might make them "authentically" grassroots, but it doesn't help them be effective. As Stoughton activist Sarah Streed asks: "What if towns and cities in Wisconsin did not have to reinvent the wheel each time they were approached by Wal-Mart? What if we had a statewide organization that any town or city could contact at the first overture? When the Wal-Mart threat rears its head, a town or city could immediately plug into a statewide organization that could quickly respond in the most effective manner instead of having to make it up as it goes."[26]

So what's the point? To put it bluntly: pick your battles. As painful as it might be to concede, in urban areas with bleak jobs prospects and few places to buy so much as a fresh tomato, Wal-Mart probably isn't worth fighting at all. How does one convince an alderman from the deindustrialized West Side of Chicago that a

Supercenter is worse than chronic unemployment? In this sort of scenario, Wal-Mart may actually be, well, a good thing, or at least a very necessary evil.

In other places, taking part in a community struggle can be a transforming experience. A common criticism of many of the new exurban developments is their tendency to isolate. In the sprawling new exurbs, people work, shop, and reproduce in islands bridged only by county roads. Privacy and comfort are undeniably popular facets of American life. But they have yet to completely suppress a deeper need for community. In the early nineties, developers surveyed home buyers about the amenities they were looking for. They listed luxury items like golf courses. A decade worth of "golf communities" later, a similar survey found a shift toward things like walking paths, parks, and, yes, even Starbucks.

Fighting off a Supercenter is no one's idea of a block party, but faced with a threat to their quality of life, to say nothing of their single biggest investment, their house, people come together in ways more profound than at the average weenie roast. Site fights also dispute the construct of Wal-Mart as a good neighbor. That so many of its stores are contested, in states red, blue, and swing, should be food for thought: Why do its traffic studies so often contain misleading data? If Wal-Mart is so sure it has the support of "a silent majority," why does it never poll the public? Why does it not attempt to talk with the people who disagree rather than write them off immediately as irrational Wal-Mart haters or radical preservationists? When alternative sites are suggested, sites that won't inspire the same traffic problems or affect surrounding real estate, why does it stand its ground like a die-hard Confederate?

"This whole experience has started to radicalize me at the young age of fifty-three," says John Myers, attorney for the Southwest Springfield Neighbors Association. Of course he's still a Republican;

but when people ask about the discrepancy, he smiles and says, "I'm a Teddy Roosevelt Republican."[27]

Sue Hines of West Springfield puts it this way: "Hey, I'm not going to deny them [Wal-Mart] business. If they want to set up, there's plenty of land a few miles west and there's only a bank and a Cingular West office, be my guest. I've worked myself to death trying to get two kids through junior high school, and college. I don't want my property value to go down fifty thousand dollars. I pay three thousand a year in property taxes—do you think *they're* going to go down if the store goes in?"[28]

Hardly the polemics of a modern-day Emma Goldman. And yet to people in a conservative city like Springfield, the aftertaste of a site fight does not bode well for Wal-Mart.

"I didn't start off with any major ax to grind about them, but dealing with this situation . . . has really impacted my views," Hines's neighbor Roger Kanerva says. "I've dealt with many hundreds of companies in my thirty-three-plus years as an environmental regulator in two states and have seen all types of good and bad actors along the way. I have developed a pretty good radar for these sorts of things, and it tells me that this bunch is bad news. It may sound a bit corny but I'm coming around to seeing Wal-Mart as a huge company without a 'heart' in the business sense. It's one thing to show a hard-nosed style in pursuit of your aims and an entirely different matter to cross the line into a ruthless sort of determination to have your way at whatever cost to the community."[29]

Wal-Mart doesn't disclose such information, but if the history of its growth offers any indication, then chances are good that bitter site fights do not translate into low-performing stores. The resentment and bitterness in the fight's aftermath is seldom outsourced to Bentonville. Instead, it festers within a community. What's the cost of enraging a few hundred neighbors, lowering the resale value of a few surrounding homes, adding another 10,000 car trips each day? Chances are it's a lot less than the $100 million the average Supercenter will do year in and year out.

The problem, though, is that when Wal-Mart busts into town, the competition—if any is left—has to do something to compete, and often that something is slashing wages. The Los Angeles City Council commissioned a report during its site fight that found the presence of Supercenters result in diminished wages among surrounding retailers. This trend led, in turn, to greater reliance on public services. The report, prepared by the consulting firm Rodino and Associates, recommended to the city council that it refuse Wal-Mart the right to build any Supercenters in Los Angeles—that is, unless the company promised to increase its wages and employee benefits.[30]

A week after the 2004 presidential elections, CNBC aired a two-hour documentary titled *The Age of Wal-Mart*. In it, Lee Scott dismissed the hundreds of site fights across the country as the efforts of "a vocal minority." Preferring skeptical facial expressions to skeptical questioning, CNBC reporter David Faber never pressed Scott to explain why these so-called minorities have dogged Wal-Mart in every state it does business in for more than a decade, or why so many of them have prevailed. Given the chance to launch unobstructed talking points on national television, Scott deflected questions concerning people's legitimate beefs with how Wal-Mart operates, with a backhanded Machiavellian triumphalism: "Go and look at our stores that opened in places where we met opposition and ask, 'Is it that the customers didn't want us or is it that a small group didn't want us?'"

Maybe Scott's right. As long as the parking lots are full and the registers blipping, why should he care what people think?

For many, the United States of Wal-Mart is the logical outgrowth of technological innovation, supply-chain wizardry, and a corporate culture united by a vision of perpetual cost-cutting efficiencies. Consumers get the low prices they want on an ever-expanding array of products and services, Wal-Mart shores up its market share and economy of scale, and thousands of stockholders get their just deserts. What's not to like?

We may hate ourselves for loving it, or love ourselves for hating it, or simply scorn the millions who don't seem to care. But while we wring our hands and fill our carts, the corpses pile up: another grocery chain bites the dust, leaving consumers with fewer choices and workers with one less place to apply for a job. A small city's trademark company shifts production to China, displacing hundreds of workers and a town's entire identity. Union contracts, which once symbolized wage-and-benefits packages capable of supporting a modest but respectable lifestyle become increasingly meaningless as Wal-Mart's looming presence offers employers all the excuse they need to demand concessions.

ELEVEN

LAND OF THE WHITE, BLUE, AND YOU

t's one thing for a woman in Manhattan to refuse to go into a Starbucks to protest the company's homogenizing effect on historic neighborhoods; she can just as easily get her coffee at the corner bodega. It's quite another to ask millions of working-class people to stop patronizing a store that stocks everything—*everything*—on their shopping lists, at lower prices.

What's a realistic solution? Big-box abstentionism? Quit your job as an accountant and become an angry investigative journalist, turning over rocks to bring the giant to its knees? Picket every Wal-Mart in a ten-mile radius of your home? Ask poor folks to shop at the organic greengrocer a forty-five-minute bus ride from their homes instead of at the Wal-Mart that stocks fresh produce at low prices two blocks away? Some say that rather than asking consumers to stop shopping at Wal-Mart, we should be asking Wal-Mart to simply be a better company.

In May of 2004, Andrew Stern, president of the Service Employees International Union, convened a meeting with union leaders, academics, and leaders of nonprofit and community groups to discuss Wal-Mart—not how to unionize it, but how to get the company to change. One of the goals of the meeting was to formulate a set of principles (the *New York Times* likened the principles to South Africa's Sullivan principles[1]) that would lay out wage and worker-treatment guidelines.

It's a good start, but the problem is that for now there is no clearcut solution. As much as Wal-Mart's detractors like to cast it as a vicious, heartless company with no redeeming value, this simply isn't true for millions of people who are thankful to have a job, who are grateful to be able to buy fresh meat and produce in a neighborhood other grocers have been too afraid to enter, and who are pleased to find that they can buy much more for less. And as much as Wal-Mart's champions like to heap praise upon the Bentonville crew for creating a distinctly American company that has managed to cut costs to the bone while reaping record profits, the truth is that Wal-Mart is often an irresponsible and unresponsive neighbor, a reckless sprawler, a callous, miserly boss, and a whirling dervish of spin. As such, Wal-Mart is a lot like the country where it was born—a little good, a little bad, a lot confusing.

HIT 'EM WHERE IT HURTS

One fail-safe way to get the attention of Americans is to talk to them about their money, and where it all goes. One organizing principle that seems to have been underused is the fact that Wal-Mart's labor practices, in particular, are costing taxpayers a nice chunk of change. The Democratic staff of the Committee on Education and the Workforce released a report in early 2004 that estimated that a single 200-employee Wal-Mart costs you and your fellow taxpayers an average of half a million dollars a year. That's a single Wal-Mart. According to the report (quoted directly here), the cost of that single Wal-Mart breaks down this way:[2]

- $36,000 a year for free and reduced lunches for just 50 qualifying Wal-Mart families
- $42,000 a year for Section 8 housing assistance, assuming 3 percent of the store employees qualify for such assistance, at $6,700 per family
- $125,000 a year for federal tax credits and deductions for low-income families, assuming 50 employees are heads of household with a child and 50 are married with two children
- $100,000 a year for additional Title I expenses, assuming fifty Wal-Mart families qualify with an average of two children
- $108,000 a year for the additional federal health care costs of moving into state children's health insurance programs . . . assuming 30 employees with an average of two children qualify
- $9,750 a year for the additional costs for low income energy assistance

"Because Wal-Mart fails to pay sufficient wages," Representative George Miller of California writes, "U.S. taxpayers are forced to pick up the tab. In this sense, Wal-Mart's profits are not made only on the backs of its employees—but on the [back] of every U.S. taxpayer."[3]

In response to the Wal-Mart problem, Representative Miller and Senator Edward Kennedy introduced HR 3619 in 2004, a bill titled the Employee Free Choice Act. With more than 130 cosponsors, it offers a considerable reform of America's labor laws, making it easier for workers to unionize.

"The success of a business need not come at the expense of workers and their families," Miller writes. "Such short-sighted profit-making strategies ultimately undermine our economy. . . . Wal-Mart's current behavior must not be allowed to set the standard for American labor."[4]

THE LAST FRONTIER: NEW YORK CITY

In December of 2004, word leaked to the New York press that Wal-Mart was planning to open a 135,000-square-foot store in Rego Park, Queens, that would employ 300 people. The news came as a shock to borough and civic leaders, who told the *Queens Tribune* that they had not heard of the plans.

"They have blazed a path of economic and social destruction in towns across the U.S.," Representative Anthony Weiner told the *Tribune*. "Wal-Mart, simply put, is wrong for New York, and wrong for New Yorkers."[5]

Sound familiar?

"Wal-Mart should expect significant opposition," the director of the Downtown Brooklyn Council told the New York *Daily News*.[6] It seems it did: the store in question wasn't slated to open until 2008.

Mayor Michael Bloomberg supported Wal-Mart's plans to push into the New York metropolitan area. Sounding like the most polished Wal-flack, he told listeners to his weekly radio address that "the public votes with their dollars."[7] Mia Masten, a spokeswoman for Wal-Mart, said: "This is about customer choice. Ultimately it's the customers who decide where they shop."[8]

But the issue of whether or not to allow Wal-Mart into Queens was not set before the voters, with or without their dollars. Instead, the company would have to go through a land-use approval process, a review by the local community board, and reviews by the Queens borough president and the City Planning Commission. The city council would likely get its chance at Wal-Mart, too, if the store required zoning variances. The chairwoman of the city council's land-use committee warned Wal-Mart that "there is a large coalition of council members who are going to have some issues with the project."[9]

The president of the New York City Central Labor Council, Brian M. McLaughlin, told the *New York Times* that diverse interests were already mobilizing against the company's move into Queens, including small businesses, immigrant advocates, the NAACP, labor unions, and even religious organizations. "We think Wal-Mart is a thread that links us all together," he said. "Wal-Mart is a buzzword for indecency."[10]

And yet, indecent or not, even in New York City there are some people who wanted a Wal-Mart in their 'hood. "They're going to do well," a Queens doctor told the *Times* reporter. "People in this neighborhood all shop at the store that offers the best price. They don't have that much loyalty."[11]

Regardless, it seemed like a major site fight was on the docket, New York style. All eyes would be on Gotham because, even more so than with its beachhead in Los Angeles, if Wal-Mart can manage to penetrate the ANWR of Wal-Mart–free America, then maybe we really can be considered the United States of Wal-Mart, and short of a civil war, it may become a union that can never be torn asunder.

Then, in late February 2005, Wal-Mart, as the New York *Daily News* headlined it, got the boot in Queens. The rumble had barely begun before the owner of the proposed Wal-Mart site got nervous and ended negotiations. Sources told the *Daily News* that the real estate company, Vornado Realty Trust, changed its mind because of the anticipated opposition. Although a Wal-flack said the company would look at other sites in the city, the message was clear.

"New York is one tough customer," McLaughlin said. "If you want to do business with us, you must clean up your act."[12]

BIG-BOX AMBIVALENCE

America has long had a paradoxical relationship with its supersized self. Our biggest, most iconic brands act as our unelected global ambassadors; and yet they're ridiculed in direct proportion to their magnitude. Bart Simpson prances through a mall where every third store has become a Starbucks. *Adbusters* magazine rips corporate imagery, and films like *Fight Club* (with name-brand stars like Brad Pitt) lament the spiritual poverty of corporate consumerism.

Perhaps our collective ambivalence to big box is summed up in Nora Ephron's hideous film *You've Got Mail.* It's the story of an independent bookseller, played by Meg Ryan, whose twee little bookshop on the Upper West Side of Manhattan is struggling to compete against a new Barnes & Noble–style superstore. Surfing the Internet (still novel in 1998), she inadvertently falls for the man whose chain is destroying her livelihood. Initially Ryan's character tries to fight the good fight, as her business is part neighborhood institution and part family legacy. But even in a city teeming with Catholics and Jews, guilt is not a viable business model. After a pathetic attempt at resistance, Ryan learns to stop worrying and love the behemoth because, well, he's good with kids, has a golden retriever, and what else can she do? If you can't beat 'em, boink 'em.

You've Got Mail is a carnival of pseudosophisticated posturing and insultingly overt product placement. Its suggestion that a love affair is a merchant's best bulwark against big-box obsolescence is offensively sugarcoated, even by Hollywood's offensively sugarcoated standards. But tough as it might be to stomach, the "What can you do?" shrug is not Nora Ephron's cop-out alone. Like it or not, we live in the United States of Wal-Mart because millions of consumers elect to spend money there, lots of it, all the time. Arguing that it's only the result of deceptive marketing or imperial growth is to deny that consumers have minds of their own.

When shoppers go to Wal-Mart for a toaster or a pair of Faded Glory jeans, it's hard to claim they're consciously endorsing the flight of American jobs overseas or the erosion of wages and benefits for workers at surrounding stores. It's not as if Wal-Mart, or any other discounter, educates its customers on the consequences of our purchases. There's no equivalent to a "Surgeon General's Warning" stickered to products from factories in China and Bangladesh, where labor laws are virtually nonexistent; there's no published roster of local businesses being muscled out, or a tally of Wal-Mart employees whose wages require them to sign on for public assistance.

But even if thousands of "fair trade" Supercenters were to bloom overnight, would we be willing to pay a premium for social responsibility? Would we be willing to put humanistic values before low prices? And if so, for how long? Asking others, and ourselves, to think of sweatshops instead of cute clothes, to think of struggling indigenous peoples instead of good coffee beans, to think of the thousands of uninsured Wal-Mart employees instead of the cheap baby formula on sale is about as likely to succeed as asking a teenage boy to avert his eyes from the squiggly Spice Channel when it comes in clear for a couple of seconds.

The ugly truth is that we've become a nation that values little above a bargain. Customer service, product quality, a connection to the people who make and sell our sacred stuff—it's all become secondary to savings. The cult of low prices has become so ingrained in the consumer culture that deep discounts are no longer novelties. They are entitlements. And this sense of entitlement has consequences. As long as we remain blind to those consequences, we will also remain blind to the costs we pay, not at Wal-Mart but in our own conflicted souls.

ACKNOWLEDGMENTS

We're a nation of workers, thinkers, drunkards, soldiers, musicians, gossips, athletes, volunteers, listeners, Internet lurkers, mothers, fathers, and friends. We're so much more than a mythic construct called "the consumer." We require so much more than everyday low prices. One day perhaps we'll have the courage to realize that this entitlement to "cheap" is our new crack cocaine. In the meantime, those taking on Wal-Mart on so many disparate fronts must grapple with one of the most complex social-change questions of our time: How do you convince a poor person that a $28 DVD player sucks?

Ugh.

Taming the Beast from Bentonville will require not only mass mobilization in the tradition of American protest movements, but also our most imaginative thinking. If this book contributes to anyone's solving this riddle in ways small and large, it will have been time well spent.

A thousand humble thank-yous to Jeremy P. Tarcher/Penguin for giving me this opportunity. I'm especially in the debt of my editor, Ashley Shelby, for her patience, support, and ass-busting work to turn an impressive blob of text into a real live book.

An enormous nod of gratitude to my father, Saul Dicker, for not asking "How's the book going?" as much as he would have liked; and to my mother, Ellen Dicker, for instilling me with a begrudging respect for interstate retail reconnaissance.

I was helped immeasurably by the wisdom and insights of Bill Pearson and his comrade Bernie Hesse of UFCW Local 789. I also benefited from bending the ears and picking the brains of countless others, including Timothy Mennel, Mark Engler, and Charles Fishman.

This book was researched and written in libraries public and private. To the good people of Colorado College's Tutt Library and the El Paso County and Denver public libraries: Thank you for comfortable, quiet, resource-rich places to work. (Now, what say you forgive my late fees?)

To my bestest friend, David Melito: Though I'll never match your capacity to whine, thanks for tolerating so much of mine. Thanks also to Eleanor Hickerson for listening, to Lisa Kennedy for Thanksgiving dinner on deadline, and to Noel Black for being an incurable chugger.

An extra special xx and oo to my sweetheart, Shannon Cumberland, who tolerated my foul moods, foul grooming, and the Wal-Martization of her home while keeping me clothed and fed in the throes of deadline doom. I couldn't have made it without you. (Now watch me dance!)

Oh, and a big smiley-faced thanks to Wal-Mart Stores, Inc. You continue to fascinate and astonish me while simultaneously turning my stomach. Without you this book would not have been possible.

John Dicker
Denver, Colorado
January 6, 2005

NOTES

INTRODUCTION

1. Wal-Mart Annual Report for 2004.
2. Daniel D. Barry and Kevin Bolero, "Smaller Supercenter Format to Extend Life Cycle of Supercenter," Merrill Lynch market research report no. 729 (June 24, 2004), p. F6.
3. World Gold Council National Retail Report for Jewelry Sales, 2002.
4. Charles Williams, "Supermarkets Sweepstakes: Traditional Grocery Chains Mull Responses to Wal-Mart's Growing Dominance," Charleston, S.C., *Post and Courier,* November 10, 2003.
5. "How Big Can It Grow?" *The Economist,* April 15, 2005.
6. Nelson Lichtenstein, "From General Motors to Wal-Mart: Templates for an Era," introductory presentation, University of California at Santa Barbara, April 12, 2004.

CHAPTER ONE

1. Ann Zimmerman, "Under Pressure, 'Big Box' Chains Redesign Stores," *Wall Street Journal,* April 14, 2004.
2. "How Big Can It Grow?" *The Economist,* April 15, 2004.
3. Author interview with Ira Kalish, August 11, 2004.
4. Andy Serwer, "The Malling of America," *Fortune,* October 13, 2003.
5. Robin Rusch, "Private Labels: Does Branding Matter?" brandchannel .com, May 6, 2002.
6. Joseph Garnowski, "Grocery: Survival Tactics," *Progressive Grocer,* October 15, 2004.
7. Ibid.
8. "Retailer of the Year: Costco Wholesale, You Do the Math," *Private Label Buyer,* April 2004.
9. Ibid.
10. Rob Walker, "Ol' Roy," *New York Times Magazine,* February 22, 2004.
11. Anne D. D'Innocenzio, "Wal-Mart's Town Becomes a New Address for Corporate America," Associated Press, September 22, 2003.
12. "Wal-Mart Launches New Line of Private Label Electronics," *Retail Merchandiser,* October 18, 2004.
13. Sam Walton with John Huey, *Made in America* (New York: Doubleday, 1992), p. 46.
14. Thomas Hine, *I Want That!* (New York: HarperCollins, 2002).
15. Ann Zimmerman, "Defending Wal-Mart," *Wall Street Journal,* October 6, 2004.
16. *Federal Register,* vol. 69, no. 30 (February 13, 2004), pp. 7336–38.
17. Elizabeth MacDonald, "Giant Slayer," *Forbes,* September 6, 2004.
18. Steven Greenhouse, "Labor Department Wins $1.9 Million in Back Pay for Janitors," *New York Times,* August 26, 2004. Sadly, such practices aren't limited to the house of Wal-Mart. In 2003, the Minneapolis-based Target organization eliminated health insurance for part-time associates. It also put the kibosh on "shift differential," or a wage premium, for those working the graveyard shift. A few months after Wal-Mart felt the heat on janitorial subcontracters using illegal immigrants, Target paid nearly $2 million in unpaid overtime to more than 700

immigrant janitors exploited in an arrangement nearly identical to Wal-Mart's. Insomuch as it offers a model for competitors, Wal-Mart also serves its industry as an effective buffer against bad PR.

19. Don Longo, "Fighting a Bad Rap," *Retail Merchandiser,* May 1, 2004.

20. Ibid.

21. Abigail Goldman and Nancy Cleeland, "An Empire Built on Bargains Remakes the Working World," *Los Angeles Times,* November 23, 2002.

22. "Wal-Mart's CEO on Offensive Against Critics," Associated Press, January 13, 2005.

23. "Wal-Mart's New Spin," *New York Times,* September 14, 2004.

CHAPTER TWO

1. Bob Ortega, *In Sam We Trust* (New York: Crown, 1998).

2. Sam Walton with John Huey, *Made in America* (New York: Doubleday, 1992), p. 25.

3. Ibid., p. 38.

4. Ibid.

5. Robert Slater, *The Wal-Mart Decade* (New York: Portfolio/Penguin, 2003).

6. U.S. Census for 1940. Walton graduated from the University of Missouri in 1940, the same year the U.S. census first surveyed for income.

7. Vance Trimble, *Sam Walton: The Inside Story of America's Richest Man* (New York: Dutton, 1990), p. 100.

8. Walton with Huey, *Made in America,* p. 45.

9. Michael Bergdahl, *What I Learned from Sam Walton* (Hoboken, N.J.: Wiley, 2004).

10. "Analyst Offers a Glance at Wal-Mart's Reckoning," *Arkansas Democrat Gazette,* April 29, 2001.

11. "Wal-Mart's New Spin," *New York Times,* September 14, 2004. The *New York Times* editorial took Wal-Mart CEO Lee Scott to task for comments he'd made at a Goldman Sachs retailing conference suggesting the negative press the company had received was not the result of malfeasance but merely media bias that favors accentuating the negative.

12. Trimble, *Sam Walton,* p. 143.

13. Ibid.

CHAPTER THREE

1. Bob Ortega, *In Sam We Trust* (New York: Crown, 1998), p. 268.
2. Michael Bergdahl, *What I Learned from Sam Walton* (Hoboken, N.J.: Wiley, 2004), p. 35.
3. *Is Wal-Mart Good for America? Frontline,* transcript, PBS, November 15, 2004.
4. Ann Zimmerman, "Price War on Aisle 3," *Wall Street Journal,* May 27, 2003. Figure attributed to Burt Flickinger III, a widely quoted industry expert in strategic marketing.
5. Joe Conason, *Big Lies: The Right-Wing Propaganda Machine and How It Distorts the Truth* (New York: Thomas Dunne, 2003).
6. Roland Marchand, *Creating the Corporate Soul* (Berkeley: University of California Press, 1998).
7. "Wal-Mart Seeks to Sell Its Vendors on Automation," *New York Times,* November 23, 1987.
8. Author interview with Tina Krieg, September 16, 2004.
9. In *What I Learned from Sam Walton,* former Wal-Mart executive Michael Bergdahl notes: "I believe that because of the cookie cutter nature of Wal-Mart stores the intellectual horsepower of the organization for strategy development purposes is centered in the hands of a very few smart people at the top" (pp. 146–47).
10. Nicholas Varchaver, "Scanning the Globe," *Fortune,* May 17, 2004.
11. Ortega, *In Sam We Trust,* p. 130.
12. Michael Schrage, "Wal-Mart Trumps Moore's Law," *Technology Review,* March 2002.
13. "Wal-Mart Adding Flat-Screen Monitors for In-store TV Net," *Retail Merchandiser,* November 9, 2004.
14. Paul Westerman, *Data Warehousing: Using the Wal-Mart Model* (San Francisco: Morgan Kaufman Publishers, 2001), p. 179.
15. Constance L. Hays, "What They Know About You," *New York Times,* November 14, 2004.
16. W. J. Holstein, "Data Crunching Santa," *U.S. News & World Report,* February 21, 1998, p. 44.

17. Ibid.
18. Kelly Barron, "Spamouflage and Cajun Crawtators," *Forbes,* October 29, 2001.
19. Ibid.
20. Holstein, "Data Crunching Santa," p. 44.
21. Linda Dillman, testimony before House Energy and Commerce Committee, Subcommittee on Commerce, Trade, and Consumer Protection, July 14, 2004.
22. Thomas Wailgum, "Tag, You're Late," *CIO,* November 14, 2004.
23. Matthew Boyle, "Wal-Mart Keeps the Change," *Fortune,* November 10, 2003.
24. Three of Wal-Mart's top hundred suppliers were able to wriggle their way out of the deadline, on the basis of extenuating circumstances in their businesses.
25. Dillman, testimony before House Energy and Commerce Committee.

CHAPTER FOUR

1. Elizabeth MacDonald, "Giant Slayer," *Forbes,* September 6, 2004.
2. The report from the Committee on Education and the Workforce from the U.S. House of Representatives cited claims that the average wage at Wal-Mart was $8.23 an hour, or $13,861 a year, in 2001.
3. Greta Guest, "$105 Million Awaits Former Kmart CEO," *Detroit Free Press,* October 21, 2004.
4. Steven Greenhouse, "Altering of Worker Time Cards Spurs Growing Number of Suits," *New York Times,* April 4, 2004.
5. Steven Greenhouse, "In-House Audit Says Wal-Mart Violated Labor Laws," *New York Times,* January 13, 2004.
6. Steven Greenhouse, "Suits Say Wal-Mart Forces Workers to Toil off the Clock," *New York Times,* June 25, 2002.
7. Steven Greenhouse, "Workers Assail Night Lock-Ins by Wal-Mart," *New York Times,* January 18, 2004.
8. Greg Schneider and Dina El Boghdady, "Wal-Mart Confirms Probe of Hiring," *Washington Post,* November 5, 2003.

9. "The Age of Wal-Mart: Inside America's Most Powerful Company," CNBC, November 10, 2004.

10. "Everyday Low Wages: The Hidden Price We All Pay for Wal-Mart," a report by the Democratic staff of the Committee on Education and the Workforce, U.S. House of Representatives, February 16, 2004, p. 7.

11. Ibid.

12. Bernard Wysocki, Jr., and Ann Zimmerman, "Wal-Mart Cost-Cutting Finds Big Target in Health Benefits," *Wall Street Journal,* September 30, 2003.

13. "Everyday Low Wages: The Hidden Price We All Pay for Wal-Mart." p. 7.

14. Wysocki and Zimmerman, "Wal-Mart Cost-Cutting Finds Big Target in Health Benefits."

15. Michael Hiltzik, "Wal-Mart's Costs Can't Always Be Measured," *Los Angeles Times,* February 2, 2004.

16. Arindrajit Dube and Ken Jacobs, "Hidden Cost of Wal-Mart Jobs," UC Berkeley Center for Labor Research, August 2, 2004.

17. Reed Abelson, "States Are Battling Against Wal-Mart over Health Care," *New York Times,* November 1, 2004.

18. Wisconsin Department of Health and Family Services.

19. Rebecca Ferrar, "Big Companies Have a Large Number of Workers in Program," *Knoxville News-Sentinel,* January 30, 2005.

20. Sylvia Chase, "The True Cost of Shopping at Wal-Mart," *NOW with Bill Moyers,* transcript, PBS, December 19, 2003.

21. Ibid.

22. "Wal-Mart Invests Millions in California Republicans, Corporate Ballot Initiatives," Associated Press, October 27, 2004.

23. Abelson, "States Are Battling Against Wal-Mart over Health Care."

24. "Wal-Mart Responds to Defeat of California Proposition 72," PR Newswire, November 3, 2004.

25. Ceci Connolly, "Higher Costs, Less Care; Data Show Crisis in Health Insurance," *Washington Post,* September 28, 2004. The figures came from Families USA, quoted in the story.

26. Commonwealth Fund study.

27. Dan Levine, "Wal-Mart's Big City Blues," *The Nation,* November 24, 2003.

28. Ibid.

29. Ibid.

CHAPTER FIVE

1. Author interview with Mike Leonard, September 2, 2004.

2. Liza Featherstone, *Selling Women Short: The Landmark Battle for Workers' Rights at Wal-Mart* (New York: Basic Books, 2004).

3. While reporting for the *Colorado Springs Independent* on an abortive union campaign at a Supercenter in Canon City, Colorado, the author received an e-mail from Wal-flack Sarah Williams that contained a *New York Times* article about declining union memberships. The trajectory of spin couldn't have been more obvious: workers have made a conscious decision to abandon unions. Somehow, the devastation of heavily unionized manufacturing industries and unbelievably toothless labor law doesn't fit into Wal-Mart's preferred history.

4. Author interview with Mike Leonard, September 2, 2004.

5. UFCW 2003 LM-2 statement. Available from the U.S. Department of Labor website: http://union-reports.dol.gov.

6. This information has been confirmed in separate interviews with Bill Pearson, Mike Leonard, and Jon Lehman.

7. Steven Greenhouse and Charlie LeDuff, "Grocery Workers Relieved, If Not Happy, at Strike's End," *New York Times,* February 28, 2004.

8. "Everyday Low Wages: The Hidden Price We All Pay for Wal-Mart," a report by the Democratic staff of the Committee on Education and the Workforce, U.S. House of Representatives, February 16, 2004, p. 5.

9. "Taking on Wal-Mart," *Socialist Worker Online*, June 25, 2004.

10. "Everyday Low Wages: The Hidden Price We All Pay for Wal-Mart."

11. Janet Forgrieve, "Hillary Clinton Praises Retailers, Cites Challenges," *Rocky Mountain News,* January 13, 2004.

12. "The Age of Wal-Mart: Inside America's Most Powerful Company," CNBC, November 10, 2004.

13. Peter T. Kilborn, "Wal-Mart's 'Buy American,'" *New York Times,* April 10, 1985.

14. Alex Daniels, "Clothier Reaps from Walton's Ideas," *Arkansas Democrat-Gazette,* October 10, 2004.

15. Ibid.

16. Ibid. This story noted that while Farris Fashions is still supplying Wal-Mart, its volume has shrunk down to a quarter of what it was at its 1996 peak.

17. Bob Ortega, *In Sam We Trust* (New York: Crown, 1998), pp. 224–25.

18. Ibid.

19. Ellen Neuborne, "Ad Support for Wal-Mart Swells," *USA Today,* January 12, 1993.

20. "Fumble, Then Recovery: The Giffords Give Cold, Hard Cash to Sweatshop Workers," New York *Daily News,* May 24, 1996.

CHAPTER SIX

1. "The Age of Wal-Mart: Inside America's Most Powerful Company," CNBC, November 10, 2004.

2. Steven Greenhouse, "In-House Audit Says Wal-Mart Violated Labor Laws," *New York Times,* January 31, 2004.

3. Thomas Friedman, *New York Times,* March 1, 2004. Globalism's most committed hyperbolist, Friedman speaks of Indian call centers and the dignity and hope they afford as an alternative to the hopelessness of the Middle East, where men yearn for martyrdom. The tenuous connection he draws assumes that jihadis are somehow coming from India. Though he floats the idea of call centers in Pakistan, which would've made the comparison more relevant, everyone he interviews over the course of several columns is Indian.

4. Doug Bandow, "Labor Activists Target Wal-Mart," *Human Events,* December 2, 2002.

5. Figures derived from the U.S. Bureau of Labor Statistics, quoted in Christian E. Weller, "The Economy Has Turned the Corner . . . into a Dead End," Center for American Progress, August 9, 2004.

6. Peter Wonacott, "Wilting Plants: Behind China's Export Boom, Heated Battle Among Factories," *Wall Street Journal,* November 13, 2003.

7. Ibid.

8. Ted C. Fishman, "The Chinese Century," *New York Times Magazine,* July 4, 2004.

9. Peter S. Goodman and Philip P. Pan, "Chinese Workers Pay for Wal-Mart's Low Prices," *Washington Post,* February 8, 2004. The figure is given as "more than 80 percent of the 6,000 factories in Wal-Mart's worldwide database of suppliers are in China."

10. Jenny Strasburg, "Gap Finds Problems at Thousands of Its Overseas Factories," *San Francisco Chronicle,* May 13, 2004.

11. Wonacott, "Wilting Plants: Behind China's Export Boom."

12. "China's Rising Rural Incomes Create Labor Shortage," *Taiwan News,* August 19, 2004.

13. A 2004 survey by *CFO* magazine found that in fact 47 percent of survey respondents said the majority of outsourced jobs paid $50,000 or more and 19 percent said 100 percent of the jobs they offshored paid $50,000 or more. See Kris Frieswick, "The Backlash," *CFO,* July 2004.

14. Loren Steffy, "We Have Seen the Job-Taking Enemy, and 'They' Are Us," *Houston Chronicle,* June 13, 2004.

15. Steve Lohr, "An Elder Challenges Outsourcing's Orthodoxy," *New York Times,* September 9, 2004.

16. "The Age of Wal-Mart."

17. Don Longo, "Fighting a Bad Rap," *Retail Merchandiser,* May 2004.

CHAPTER SEVEN

1. Wal-Mart Stores at Goldman Sachs retail conference, September 8, 2004, final transcript, Thompson Street Events.

2. Karen Blumenthal, "Arrival of Discounter Tears the Civic Fabric of Small-Town Life," *Wall Street Journal,* April 14, 1987.

3. Hugh Sidey, "The Two Sides of the Sam Walton Legacy," *Time,* April 20, 1992.

4. John Bowermaster, "When Wal-Mart Comes to Town," *New York Times Magazine,* April 2, 1989.

5. Sidey, "The Two Sides of the Sam Walton Legacy."

6. Sam Walton with John Huey, *Made in America* (New York: Doubleday, 1992), p. 178.

7. Ibid.

8. George Will, "Waging War on Wal-Mart," *Newsweek,* July 5, 2004.

9. Jay Nordlinger, "The New Colossus," *National Review,* April 2004.

10. Luke Boggs, *Human Events,* April 12, 2004.

11. Jeanne Cummings, "Joining the PAC: Wal-Mart Opens for Business in a Tough Market," *Wall Street Journal,* March 24, 2004.

12. "Wal-Mart Becomes the Largest Corporate Investor," *Financial Times,* February 24, 2004.

13. Scott does not usually mention how the company and its lobbyists have been trying to break into the banking-services industry for the better part of the last ten years.

14. "Everyday Low Wages: The Hidden Price We All Pay for Wal-Mart," a report by the Democratic staff of the Committee on Education and the Workforce, U.S. House of Representatives, February 16, 2004, p. 15.

CHAPTER EIGHT

1. Tim LaHaye and Jerry B. Jenkins, *Glorious Appearing* (Wheaton, Ill.: Tyndale House, 2004), p. 226.

2. Allison Ballard, "Where Sparks Fly, Look for Nicholas," Wilmington, N.C., *Star News*, June 24, 2004.

3. Matt Smith, "Censorship for Dummies," *SF Weekly,* July 24, 2004.

4. Ibid.

5. Harold Meyerson, "Protocols of Wal-Mart," *The American Prospect,* November 2004.

6. "Wal-Mart Not Carrying 'America,'" *Publishers Weekly,* October 25, 2004.

7. Meyerson, "Protocols of Wal-Mart."

8. An NPR spokeswoman claimed that 56 percent of its listeners identified themselves as Wal-Mart shoppers, as compared with 66 percent of the American public. See "Wal-Mart Tries to Shine Its Image by Supporting Public Broadcasting," *New York Times,* August 16, 2004.

9. Leigh Gallagher, "Holy Influence," *Forbes,* December 8, 2003.

10. Ibid.

11. Richard Harrington, "Wal-Mart Halts Sale of Rock Magazines," *Washington Post,* July 17, 1986.

12. "Rock Magazines Being Removed from Wal-Mart," United Press International, July 12, 1986.

13. Ibid.

14. Marie Louise McCrory, "Pregnant Barbie in Growing Demand," *Irish Times,* April 26, 2003.

15. Jennifer Netherby and Suzanne Ault, "Docs Galore—Ditto Concerns," *Video Business News,* September 6, 2004. A video store owner in Odessa, Texas, told *Video Business News* that his shop was keeping Moore's film behind the counter, selling it only to those who asked.

16. "Everyday Low Wages: The Hidden Price We All Pay for Wal-Mart," a report by the Democratic staff of the Committee on Education and the Workforce, U.S. House of Representatives, February 16, 2004, p. 19.

17. Such was the case in Lancaster County, Pennsylvania, in the early 1990s, when union construction workers actually lobbied on Wal-Mart's behalf. In its bid for a Supercenter on Chicago's West Side, the company agreed to hire union construction firms.

CHAPTER NINE

1. From House bill quoted in William I. Walsh, *The Rise and Decline of the Great Atlantic and Pacific Tea Company* (Secaucus, N.J.: Lyle Stuart, 1986).

2. "George & John Hartford: Among the Culls, the Flipmagilders," *Time,* November 13, 1950.

3. Ibid.

4. Walsh, *The Rise and Decline.*

5. "George & John Hartford."

6. Ibid.

7. Carl G. Ryant, "The South and the Movement Against Chain Stores," *Journal of Southern History,* May 1973.

8. Ibid.

9. Ibid.

10. Robert McNatt and Ronald Grover, "Who Says Wal-Mart Is Bad for Cities?" *BusinessWeek,* February 10, 2004.

11. These numbers were attributed to Wal-Mart spokesman Keith Morris in Kristina Nwazota, "Challenging Wal-Mart," PBS Online *NewsHour,* August 20, 2004.

12. Wal-Mart community affairs manager Glen Wilkins quoted in Sarah Jane Tribble, "Fort Mill, S.C., Opponents Scoff at Wal-Mart's Plans," *Charlotte Observer,* July 23, 2004.

13. Liza Featherstone, *Selling Women Short* (New York: Basic, 2004), p. 55.

14. Emek Basker, "Job Creation or Destruction? Labor-Market Effects of Wal-Mart Expansion," working paper, University of Missouri, January 2004 (http://www.missouri.edu/~baskere/papers/WalMart.pdf).

15. "Mexican Traditionalists Fight Wal-Mart Close to Pyramids," Knight Ridder, October 29, 2004.

CHAPTER TEN

1. Erin Aubry Kaplan, "Duped by Wal-Mart," *LA Weekly,* April 2, 2004.

2. Tim Sullivan, "Manifest Destiny," *High Country News,* June 24, 2004.

3. Ibid.

4. *The Tavis Smiley Show,* NPR, transcript, March 31, 2004.

5. Erin Aubry Kaplan, "Wal-Mart's Blackout," *LA Weekly,* April 9, 2004.

6. "Wal-Mart Watch," Inner City Press website (www.innercitypress.org/wal-mart.html).

7. John M. Binder, "California Voters Reject Wal-Mart Initiative," *New York Times,* April 7, 2004.

8. "Christmas Will Come Early," *Mass Market Retailers,* 2004.

9. Greg Krupa, "Groceries Cost More for the Poor: Dearth of Inner City Supermarkets Limits Choices," *Detroit News,* August 21, 2001.

10. Matt Pulle, "Unlikely Adversaries," *Nashville Scene,* March 11, 2004.

11. Ibid.

12. Kaplan, "Wal-Mart's Blackout."

13. Jay Nordlinger, "The New Colossus," *National Review,* April 19, 2004.

14. Author interview with Sue Kuhl, November 8, 2004.

15. Author interview with Jim Hardin, October 18, 2004.

16. Author interview with John Myers, October 21, 2004.

17. Quote attributed to Wal-Mart spokesman Eric Berger in Kristina Nwazota, "Challenging Wal-Mart," PBS Online *NewsHour,* August 20, 2004.

18. David R. Anderson, "Wal-Mart Foes Hone Tactics," Portland *Oregonian,* June 29, 2003.

19. "Oregon Court of Appeals Rules Against Wal-Mart," Portland *Oregonian,* July 12, 2004.

20. Author interview with Kevin Pomeroy, November 9, 2004.

21. Leslie "Buzz" Davis, "Wal-Mart Threatens Our Way of Life, Must Be Unionized," *Capital Times,* September 1, 2003.

22. Author interview with Roger Kanerva, November 9, 2004.

23. Author interview with Jim Hardin, October 18, 2004.

24. Jim Hightower, "Winning Against Wal-Mart," *The Nation,* March 4, 2002.

25. "Christine Augustine from Bear Stearns and Steve Pearlstein with the *Washington Post* Discuss Movement Against Wal-Mart Expansion," *Kudlow & Cramer,* CNBC, September 1, 2004.

26. Sarah Streed, "Supercoalition," Fightingbob.com, April 15, 2004 (http://www.fightingbob.com/article.cfm?articleID=202).

27. Author interview with John Myers, October 21, 2004.

28. Author interview with Sue Hines, November 9, 2004.

29. Author interview with Roger Kanerva, November 9, 2004.

30. Nancy Cleeland, "City Report Is Critical of Wal-Mart Supercenters," *Los Angeles Times,* December 6, 2003.

CHAPTER ELEVEN

1. Steven Greenhouse, "Some Critics of Wal-Mart Joining Forces to Change It," *New York Times,* May 12, 2004.

2. "Everyday Low Wages: The Hidden Price We All Pay for Wal-Mart," a report by the Democratic staff of the Committee on Education and

the Workforce, U.S. House of Representatives, February 16, 2004, p. 9.

3. Ibid.

4. Ibid., p. 21.

5. "Foes Blast Plan to Bring Wal-Mart to Rego Park," *Queens Tribune,* December 26, 2004.

6. Lore Croghan, "Wal-Mart Eyes Brooklyn Site," New York *Daily News,* December 20, 2004.

7. William Murphy, "Mayor Gives Nod to Queens Wal-Mart," New York *Newsday,* December 17, 2004.

8. Curtis L. Taylor, "Wal-Mart Should Expect a Fight in Queens," New York *Daily News,* December 21, 2004.

9. Ibid.

10. Jennifer 8. Lee, "Critics Seek to Block Plan for Wal-Mart in Queens," *New York Times,* December 17, 2004.

11. Ibid.

12. Timothy Williams, "Wal-Mart Gets the Message from NYC: No," *Chicago Sun-Times,* February 25, 2005.

RESOURCES

WEBSITES

- Wal-Mart Stores, Inc: www.walmart.com
  Home of Rollback Smiley. Buy, buy, buy!

- Wal-Mart vs. Women: www.walmartvswomen.com
  Watchdog group keeping tabs on Wal-Mart's treatment of female employees.

- Wal-Mart Class-Action Website: www.walmartclass.com
  Website dedicated to tracking the progress of the *Dukes vs. Wal-Mart* class-action lawsuit.

- Sprawl-Busters: www.sprawl-busters.com
  An international clearinghouse on big-box antisprawl information, with a great list of recommended reading and tips on how to keep a behemoth out of your backyard. Also home of anti–Wal-Mart legend Al Norman.

- International Forum on Globalization: www.ifg.org
  An alliance of sixty leading activists, scholars, economists, researchers, and writers formed to stimulate new thinking, joint activity, and public education in response to economic globalization. Remember the Seattle WTO protests? Yeah, them.

- Center for Justice and Democracy: www.centerjd.org
  A nonprofit, nonpartisan public-interest organization that works to educate the public about the importance of the civil justice system and the dangers of so-called "tort reforms," which would put lawsuits like *Dukes vs. Wal-Mart* and the *Exxon Valdez* damages suit in danger of ever going forward, leading to a giant vacuum where corporate accountability used to be.

- United Food and Commercial Workers Union: www.ufcw.org
  Home of the UFCW, with updated information about its attempts to unionize Wal-Mart.

- Fairness & Accuracy In Reporting (FAIR): www.fair.org
  National media watchdog group. Despite Sam Walton's distaste for all things media, we get a sanitized view of corporate activity due to the fact that the major networks and newspapers in this country are, well, corporate.

- Center for Media and Democracy: www.prwatch.org
  A nonprofit watchdog group that keeps tabs on corporate media and publishes the *PR Watch* newsletter, which investigates and exposes how the public relations industry and other professional propagandists manipulate public information, perceptions, and opinion on behalf of governments and special interests.

- Institute for Local Self-Reliance: www.ilsr.org
  A nonprofit research and educational organization that provides technical assistance and information on environmentally sound economic
  development strategies for communities interested in concepts such as
  smart growth and green growth.

- Wal-Mart Sucks: http://forum.walmartsucks.com
  A great resource for Wal-Mart workers, to whom this site caters.

FURTHER READING

Beating Back Wal-Mart

Note: Of the books listed below, some of which provide advice on how to
avoid becoming a community or business killed by Wal-Mart, only two
were published by large publishing houses.

- *Selling Women Short: The Landmark Battle for Workers' Rights at Wal-Mart*
  by Liza Featherstone (Basic Books, 2004)

- *The Hometown Advantage: How to Defend Your Main Street Against Chain
  Stores and Why It Matters* by Stacy Mitchell (Institute for Local Self-
  Reliance, 2000)

- *The Case Against Wal-Mart* by Al Norman (Raphael Marketing, 2004)

- *Slam-Dunking Wal-Mart* by Al Norman (Raphael Marketing, 1999)

- *In Sam We Trust: The Untold Story of Sam Walton and Wal-Mart, the World's
  Most Powerful Retailer* by Bob Ortega (Crown Business, 1998)

- *Up Against the Wal-Marts: How Your Business Can Prosper in the Shadow of
  the Retail Giants* by Don Taylor (American Management Association,
  1996)

Know Thine Enemy (or Thy Hero—
It Depends on Your Point of View)

Note: All of these laudatory books were published by large publishing houses, including the courageous John Wiley & Sons.

- *Sam Walton: Made in America* by Sam Walton with John Huey (Doubleday, 1992)

- *The Wal-Mart Triumph: Inside the World's #1 Company* by Robert Slater (Portfolio/Penguin, 2004)

- *What I Learned from Sam Walton: How to Compete and Thrive in a Wal-Mart World* by Michael Bergdahl (John Wiley & Sons, 2004)

INDEX

ABOUT THE AUTHOR

John Dicker is a writer based in Denver. His work has appeared in *The Nation, Salon,* and numerous alternative newsweeklies. *The United States of Wal-Mart* is his first book.